THE LAST LAYER OF
THE OCEAN

THE LAST LAYER OF THE OCEAN

Kayaking through Love and Loss on Alaska's Wild Coast

Mary Emerick

Oregon State University Press Corvallis

Library of Congress Cataloging-in-Publication Data
Names: Emerick, Mary, author.
Title: The last layer of the ocean : kayaking through love and loss on Alaska's wild coast /
    Mary Emerick.
Other titles: Kayaking through love and loss on Alaska's wild coast
Description: Corvallis : Oregon State University Press, 2021.
Identifiers: LCCN 2020057154 | ISBN 9780870710797 (trade paperback) |
    ISBN 9780870710810 (ebook)
Subjects: LCSH: Emerick, Mary. | Alexander Archipelago (Alaska)—Description and
    travel. | Baranof Island (Alaska)—Biography. | Forest rangers—Alaska—Tongass National
    Forest—Biography. | Tongass National Forest (Alaska) | Sea kayaking—Alaska—Alaska,
    Gulf of. | Alaska, Gulf of (Alaska)—Description and travel. | Man-woman
    relationships—Alaska—Baranof Island.
Classification: LCC F912.A19 E44 2021 | DDC 917.980—dc23
LC record available at https://lccn.loc.gov/2020057154

♾ This paper meets the requirements of ANSI/NISO Z39.48-1992
    (Permanence of Paper).

First published in 2021 by Oregon State University Press
Printed in the United States of America

Oregon State University
OSU Press

Oregon State University Press
121 The Valley Library
Corvallis OR 97331-4501
541-737-3166 • fax 541-737-3170
www.osupress.oregonstate.edu

*Dedicated to the kayak partners
who traveled with me on the wild Alaska coast.
You will never be forgotten.*

Although all the events depicted in this memoir are true, some have been consolidated or the timeline moved for clarity. Most nonhistoric names have been changed except for a few: Audrey Sutherland, Billy from Nondalton, and Eric, who disappeared in a Beaver floatplane. Although "Helga" represents my usual kayaking partner, she is also a composite of others who joined me on the high seas.

Chapter 2 of the "Ferry" section appeared in slightly different form in the online journal *Rise Forms* in 2013.

Contents

launch

You might think that launching is the easiest part of sea kayaking—at least, easier than being far from shore, where many things could happen. But in this, you would be wrong. It can be the hardest part, because moving from land to sea takes more effort than you realize. Land is familiar, where humans belong. We can't breathe in water, not for long anyway, and the ocean has layers like a cake, each zone darker and deeper than the one before. When you launch, you commit to the paddle. You are moving from a place of safety to one where everything is uncertain. Make sure this is what you really want.

I understood the kind of people that I came from but not why I felt so different from them. They were generations of people who had searched for home, found the one place that spoke to them, and stayed. Like aspens, their roots went deep below the surface, connecting to other groups of people, an invisible skein of connection that I had never been able to master.

My grandfather and later my father were named after the land, the most important thing there was, though they pronounced their name, Lando, with a long *ah* instead of a flat *a*. They were descendants of Indiana farmers, and the land meant everything to them: nourishment, comfort, livelihood. Like his ancestors, my father cultivated a deep tie to place, settling in a remote, snow-battered town in northern Michigan. He watched in bemusement as I prepared to escape the place he loved. I didn't understand this kind of tie. Instead I was propelled by an invisible force, an unseen hand at my back.

I had always known I was different. There was a restlessness inside me that threatened to surge out of my skin. It pushed me to keep moving, even when each place I discovered was good enough for everyone else. I was always tapping my foot, fidgeting, casting off each landscape and each man that threatened to tie me down. There had to be somewhere else, somewhere better, just around the curve of that mountain road, down along that river valley. I drove across the country barefoot, windows down, breathing in new air.

I had always kept anyone who could have loved me at an impenetrable distance. If I let them in, I reasoned, it would break my heart to leave, and I knew I would always leave. Plus, if they really knew me, how different I was, would they really want me to stay? The voices of the men I had left behind echoed in my thoughts, even after I turned the radio up higher to drown them out.

"You had one foot out the door the whole time."

"I hope you find what you're looking for."

"What did I do wrong?"

≈

I knew I was leaving a series of wounded hearts in my wake, but I couldn't seem to stop. It didn't take long—six months, a year—before I was packing up to leave again. It had been five years in my current town, a lifetime. It was time to go.

I was thirty-eight and had quit everywhere I had tried. I had lived in ten states, moving restlessly in a seasonal migration from west to east and back again, working temporary jobs in national parks and forests. The list of jobs was long: naturalist, firefighter, biological technician, park fee collector, campground worker, wilderness manager. I bounced back and forth to both coasts and in between: Pennsylvania, Michigan, Wisconsin, New Mexico, Nevada, Washington, Idaho, and California. There was nothing wrong with any of those places, but I couldn't stay put in any of them. The problem, I knew, was with me. I was missing something that other people seemed to have, some puzzle piece that I could not quite find. I had always felt on the outside everywhere. Nowhere felt like home, except for the road. I didn't know how I would know when I found a real home, but I knew I hadn't found it yet.

I studied the faces of those who claimed to have found their home. How did they know? Did home just sink into your bones, irrefutable? How did you decide that this was the one, the only place? Or was I being foolish, chasing something ephemeral, when in fact you just hunkered down somewhere, called it good? Made the best of it?

The town I lived in now was in the outback of eastern Oregon, perched on the shallow edge of the Great Basin. This place, where all the water was captured and held tight, unable to drain to the ocean, was just another place I could not call home. It felt alien, the cloudless sky too big, myself too small underneath it. I knew it was true: I had failed again.

It had been this way from the beginning. The neighborhood girls of my childhood, in their Dorothy Hamill wedge haircuts and clogs, had seemed to have their lives set from the start. College, marriage, babies—they had it all figured out. How were they so certain? I didn't want what they wanted. Instead I pictured myself a traveler, long braid hanging over a tanned shoulder, backpack in hand. I would climb mountain trails and run rivers. I would be the person heard from by postcards, the woman nobody could catch. What I hadn't imagined was that all the traveling never added up to the one thing I also was starting to want: the feeling of home somewhere, the place you sank deep into. Nobody else I knew seemed to wrestle with this. They traveled for a time, if they traveled at all, and then dug in, happy with their choice.

I was staring down at forty, single and childless in a remote western outpost that valued neither. The other women watched me as if they could see the thing that still tugged on my heart. There were men here, they said, good men with pickup trucks that ran, men with jobs, men who had cemented themselves into this valley. Did I want to be single forever, they asked, not a question but an observation on my fate if I didn't wise up.

These women, no-nonsense daughters of ranchers, didn't mind getting older, settling in for the long haul. Instead, they seemed as placid as the harnessed Silvies River, which meandered gently through the silver sage of our shared valley. Why I couldn't be as content as they were, sliding into middle age with a grace that eluded me, was something I could not figure out.

But I knew that the Silvies flooded sometimes, overflowing its banks in a roar of defiance. The river spread out over the land that it used to own, coaxed back into bounds eventually by the sun that sought to tame it. I knew this; I had seen it. I still believed in the possibility that you could have both, a life that included both home and adventure.

The life I had been living seemed to have an expiration date, and it was fast approaching. It was no longer acceptable to float from place to place, as rootless as the tumbleweeds that blew down Main Street in the unceasing wind. You could do that in your twenties without censure, but forty seemed too old, desperate somehow. My peers were saving for retirement, while I felt like my life had barely started. They had staying power, where I had none.

Every day in my adopted town was the same, the sky stretching in an enormous arc over the Great Basin, carved out of unyielding basalt and dry lake beds. At night, lonely husbands of other women showed up at my door, offering things: lawn mowing, fence fixing, themselves. Their eyes shone with the desperation and fear of men whose lives were passing them by. *How did I end up here?* they seemed to be asking me. *I meant for my life to be more than this. Rescue me.* I sent them packing back into the starry night to their fretful wives, looking over their shoulders to be sure I wouldn't change my mind. I understood them because I sometimes felt the same way.

≈

I drove across the state line to see a man I had once loved. I liked how Finn's aquamarine eyes crinkled at the corners and the way gray was creeping into his curly dark hair. I liked how supremely unaware he was of his combination of minuscule chopped-off jean shorts, holstered knife, hiking boots, and mangled cowboy hat, his take-me-as-I-am attitude. I had spent my life trying to pass as normal, and he stuck out like a jagged edge. Better yet, he didn't care.

Finn pushed up the sleeves of his sweatshirt and asked me whether I wanted to run the chainsaw. I was mostly an office worker now. It had been a long time since I had carried a growling Stihl saw, thirty-six-inch bar, through the forest, carefully chipping out the front wedge and slicing through the backcut to fell long-dead lodgepole trees. In the old days on a firefighting crew I had run through a tank of gas before stopping, the saw an extension of my body, nonchalant with the power of being young and strong.

Finn had been bucking up logs for his portable sawmill, and sunshine-covered sawdust coated his shoulders and hair. He even smelled like resin where the bark had rubbed off on his skin. We stood in a small clearing below a row of summer houses, shuttered up against spring. Below us the two-lane highway bisected the valley, hugging the Salmon River. If I had been tempted to stay anywhere, it would have been here, but even this place hadn't held me for long.

Finn was living a life close to the bone. He loved this valley but didn't want the anchor that would be a house, so he shifted from house-sitting gig to campground, changing his clothes in smelly vault toilets, taking baths in the icy creek. "Will you take me with you to Alaska?" he asked, when I confided that I had seen a job opening there. "You could marry me," he added, disregarding the fact that we hadn't seen each other in two years and had forgotten most of what we had ever known of each other.

Because I didn't know what to say, I yanked on the starter cord and the saw coughed once and quit. I tried it again and again until the engine flooded. The saw felt so much heavier now, my arms so weak. How had I ever done it in my firefighting days? Was this going to be the rest of my life from now on, growing older and softer in a town that felt like living on the moon?

Finn took the saw and eyed me quizzically. He squeezed my soft bicep, a muscle that had once been firm as an apple.

He had always been as unfiltered as drinking from a mountain stream. When you wanted the gut-punch truth, you got it from Finn. "What happened?" he asked. And I knew what he meant: *What happened to the girl I used to know? What have you done to yourself?*

I looked down at the dry grass under my feet. I didn't have an answer. It seemed that either you traveled forever, chasing youth and the next mountain range, or you moved into more sluggish water, thinking of all the ways you used to be. You shrugged and said to yourself that you were older, that you didn't have anything to prove, that the invisible cloak that everyone placed over middle-aged women's shoulders didn't bother you. Neither choice seemed to be the right one.

That winter the sun slid lazily lower on the horizon, and wind unimpeded hurled across the sagebrush and slammed into my house with a force that seemed personal. A crack in the ceiling spidered its way across the hallway, as if the house itself were breaking apart. I climbed on a ladder and tried to conceal it, troweling layers of spackle and paint across it, but I could still see it under all the fixes I tried. Some things, I thought, could never be repaired.

The year I made up my mind to leave, again, a woman drowned at Moon Reservoir, a handful of miles from the town of Burns. A flat sheet of blue in a brown, wrinkled landscape, Moon Reservoir had its own stark beauty. But you did not go there by accident. You had to want to get there, turn off Highway 20 deliberately onto Double O Road, a teeth-clenching route made corduroy by hundreds of summer tires. Once there you might second-guess your decision. There were no trees. The sun baked the ground into a hardpan. There was no shade or respite from the constant wind.

Rumor afterward in the tavern said that she walked around the lake filling up a backpack with rocks until it weighed forty pounds. She locked the car, put the keys in her pocket, and found the highest place. Then she jumped. Or so it was thought. Nobody would ever know what really happened.

When the troopers found the car, it was out of gas. Had she driven until it ran out and thought that this place was good enough? Did she wait for someone to come along and when nobody did, give in to despair? Moon Reservoir was not a place that people happened upon on a regular basis. You could sit out there staring through a windshield for days, long enough to pick through all of your mistakes. For months I was haunted by Moon Reservoir.

I thought of what Finn had said. I thought of all the places I had lived, all places that were fine for others but somehow not good enough for me. I made up my mind. Like countless restless souls before me, I would go to Alaska. Surely, I would find what I was looking for there. The restlessness that I could not escape would end in Alaska, letting me breathe, letting me find a home at last. Surely, Alaska would be good enough. Alaska had to be good enough. I had, finally, run out of road.

≈

"Career suicide," my supervisor said when I told him I had been offered a job in the part of Alaska nobody ever talked about, the place where the absence of rain was cause for celebration, where brown bears showed up in the neighborhoods, a place where you never wore cotton. "And you're doing what, checking outfitter permits? Really?" He shook his head and shuffled into his office.

The people I worked with were puzzled. It was less money, they pointed out, a step down the ladder from my white-collar existence of planning recreation programs. Why would anyone do that? I wasn't young anymore; I needed to think about retirement. You didn't take less; you always sought more.

The lonely husbands felt differently. I saw a flash of their younger selves when I told them. "You should definitely go," they said. "I would go if . . . ," and they shrugged, the weight of family and mortgage heavy on their rounded shoulders. Go for us, they implied but did not say. Get out while you can.

≈

Though most never knew this about me, I was plagued by an inner voice that berated me for what I perceived as weakness. I didn't know how to swim. I had never learned to ride a bike. I was afraid of bears. A constant worry dogged me, the worry that people would see through to my core and realize what I had always known: I was different. I had worked hard to hide what I had believed to be the truth, throwing myself into dangerous work on firelines and trails. I tried to prove myself over and over again, but the voice persisted. There was always something I had done wrong, some way I could have been better.

The only person I knew in all of Southeast Alaska was a friend of a friend, a man who had moved there a few months before. The thought of the ocean terrified me. I was more terrified of the life I was leaving behind. Against all rational advice, I went anyway.

forward stroke

It seems deceptively simple, but like most things, there are layers to navigate. Brute force won't get you anywhere in a small boat on the ocean. It is grace, not power, that you need to learn. The forward stroke is not exciting like the brace or elegant like the scull, but it is the stroke you will use over and over again until it is as common as breath: catch a blade full of water, pull it past you, rotate.

As the paddle rises, you do it all over again. Do this enough times and you will have traveled closer to where you want to go.

A good forward stroke is a commitment to the journey ahead. Think of it as a beginning, a clean slate. Think of it as a giant leap into the unknown.

one

The world was made of water. The whole town of Sitka revolved around water, the hungry ocean rising and falling like the breath of a giant sea creature, the rain a hammer on pavement, the rivers swollen with fat-backed salmon finding their way home. As the ferry ground to a stop at the dock, I imagined that I might be finding my way home too. Like the salmon, I had been swimming in wide circles for most of my life, and now I would live in a place where I would let myself be known. Where I might even stay. Fear and longing battled inside as I walked to meet the men who waited for me.

"This is what we call a nice day in Sitka," Sven said, gesturing expansively at the brooding clouds. A dose of sun poked tentatively through every now and then, just enough to keep a person hopeful. Steam rose from the pavement like breaths exhaled. The air contained as much moisture as a mop, and the threat of a stronger rain hovered over us. It was pouring far out in the ocean, I noticed, a dark sullen line beetling its way toward land, a curtain of rain in its wake.

After three days on the ferry, I still felt a little dizzy, as if land were the foreign territory, not water. We had chugged up the Inside Passage, through channels curving like a snake's back, a solid wall of evergreens kissing the water. It was July, the prime time for wandering. The back deck was crammed with fellow adventurers, their tents duct-taped to the metal to prevent escape. Other untamed souls slept on chaise longues in the solarium, sleeping bags draped over their bodies, backpacks bristling with outdoor gear. As we approached Sitka, two men in a skiff cut in close to the wake and mooned us before speeding off laughing.

Here in town, green-cloaked mountains rose abruptly from sea level, leaving little space for the houses that crowded the shore on a small bench of land. Some neighborhoods were carved out of sheer cliffs, houses perched precariously on the hillsides. The ocean spread flat as pancake batter as far as I could see in the other direction, dotted with small, tree-lined islands.

The sea bustled with summer activity. Skiffs buzzed in long arcs across the water, back and forth across the channel. A green and gold floatplane roared past, taking off with a shake of its wings. Boats that looked like regal old ladies steamed by, laden with nets and gear, on their way to the fishing grounds. Men with rifles over their shoulders clattered down to the docks and disappeared into smaller boats. The scene bubbled with life.

This place was nothing like the one I had left. Here it looked like nobody ever slept. This was the ceaseless mania of summer, when the days were longer than the nights, before winter dropped a curtain of darkness and isolation over the island. Things were happening, from the procession of rubber-booted men into the tavern and back out again, to the parade of camera-wielding tourists who clogged the streets. I inhaled a deep breath of fish and diesel. I knew I had made the right decision. This was the place that would change my life.

The ferry I had come on had emptied and filled again with southbound travelers. With a blast of its horn, it ponderously moved back out to sea.

Even if I had wanted to change my mind, it was too late. The next one wouldn't come for a week.

Sven and Tom, my new boss and his sidekick, were waiting on the dock as I drove my loaded Toyota off the bowels of the ferry. They lingered, waving to people they knew, in no hurry. We were on island time now. Beaming with welcome, they were an oddly matched pair—one clean-cut in jeans and fleece and hair cut in a bowl shape, the other encased in an ancient green wool jacket and the ubiquitous rubber boots everyone seemed to wear. This was, they said, the best place in the world to live.

In the office, Tom showed me my desk, neatly laid out with blank notepads, pens, and a mute computer. "Here's your outfitter-guide permits," he said, pointing to a shelf lined with brown cardboard files. "Most of them like to be called guides, not outfitters. But some do both, outfit a group with gear, or actually take people somewhere. If they take tourists to the forest, they have to have a permit to do it. There are guys who hunt bears, mostly, but also ones that take people fishing, or on little cruise ships for ten days at a time. You talk to them about where they want to take clients, and how much they charge, and then you type up their permits using this form."

He indicated an open tab on his computer: he had been typing on one of the forms before I had arrived. "Oh, and you've got the wilderness to manage also." He indicated the map hanging on our shared wall. It was clear he didn't care much about wilderness. He shrugged. "Not much happens there."

I squinted at the map, a million acres winnowed down to one oversized page. The Alexander Archipelago, the island chain on which I now lived, ran for three hundred miles, consisting of over a thousand islands clustered tight in a beefy arm of the Pacific called the Gulf of Alaska. If I traveled straight east, I would wind up in the Coast Mountains of Canada. If I went west, who knew? The map showed only a vast expanse of sea.

Baranof Island, the one I now lived on, started out fat in the north and ended up thin in the south, facing the ocean and narrowing to a sharp point at its southern tip called Cape Ommaney, where I would later witness the collision of blue-green sea around broken cliffs. You could end up waiting for days near Cape Ommaney for a favorable passage. The South Baranof Wilderness, mid-island, was a swath of jumbled mountains and coastline, stretching across the width of the island like a wide belt.

Chichagof Island, which contained the other wilderness, lay to the north, a land mass cracked nearly in half by long, fingerlike passages. Only a handful of communities perched on the outer fringes of these islands, some with no roads, only boardwalk. You could not drive to any of them. How could you even call these islands? They seemed to be entire continents, sprawling across the sea.

I was used to wildernesses I could drive to. I usually parked at a trailhead and headed onto a well-kept corridor trail that branched out across the wilderness like a remote highway. If I went off trail, I could find my way back by following the rivers that tumbled inevitably to a road outside the boundary or by scrambling over low saddles to get a bird's eye on the situation. In all but the most remote places, you could tell where other people had been. They left small circles of blackened stones, footprints, trees chopped heedlessly for firewood. There, people took possession of the forest.

These wildernesses, in contrast, had teeth. I could tell that by the busy contour lines; nothing flat and easy here. A few trails ventured in, but not far. Lost in one of these wildernesses, you could stumble around for weeks.

Tom noticed me looking at the map. "Most people never get off the beach fringe," he said. "The mountains are steep and wet, and there are plenty of bears. Mostly the tourists use guides if they want to go out there." It was too much to take in. I turned my attention back to the guide permits.

"Well, how do you check on these guides? You know, to see if they're doing what they're supposed to be doing?"

Tom shrugged. "They turn in reports at the end of the year. And then there's the ranger boat trips," he said. "Once a year, maybe twice. You can check on them then." His phone rang and he swiveled in his ergonomic desk chair, ready to get back to work.

I had heard about those trips. We would be leaving on one soon. Five people sardined into a seventy-five-foot boat, sharing an unreliable bathroom and one tiny bunk room. If the bathroom, or head, failed, you used a bucket, hoping your colleagues had the sense to stay off the deck while you were out there. Using skiffs with outboards, the workers ventured on typical ocean routes to check permits, returning each night to the boat. The ranger boat captain planned and cooked the meals, expecting no argument or vegetarians. There was no camping onshore, no real deviation from a set plan.

As a past wilderness ranger, I had learned how important it was to spend time on the land. Sleeping outdoors in a tent for a handful of nights at a time, I had seen how different a landscape became as dusk slanted across it. I had heard the night howls of distant wolves, wolves that officials would not admit were really there. I had learned where the elk yarded up in the evenings and where they spread out like a dark fan over the sagebrush valleys. I had seen the way the rivers rose during the day and calmed at night. You had to be out there to gain this kind of knowing. You didn't sleep on a boat.

Don't make waves. You're a newcomer. I stared at my computer screen. The permit form was incomprehensible, with grayed-out boxes I was supposed to fill in. Use area? Service days? I glanced at the handwritten itinerary a guide had brought in. *Myriads*, I read. *Klokachef. Slocum Arm.* What were all these places, and how would I ever know them?

Tom was deep in conversation with someone who thought it would be a good idea to build a zip line on the forest. "Well, you need to show that there's no private land available," he said. He sounded like he had said this many times before. I could hear a raised voice on the other end.

I traced the coastlines of the two large islands, Baranof and Chichagof, scalloped like lace along the edges. There were lakes nestled deep in the mountains, with names like Diana and Ekaterina and Goon Dip. There were hundreds of bays and only a handful of trail miles. Sven had told me that costs were prohibitive for trails here in this wet, unforgiving environment. A million dollars a mile was not out of the question. Most people, he said, echoing Tom, did not venture beyond the beach fringe—the first layer of forest just past the shoreline. The rainy weather and the big bears kept them out, he said, not to mention the terrain, slick and unforgiving at best, brushy and complicated at other times. The maps were only a suggestion of what really existed; some of them had never been ground truthed.

My predecessor had bought a couple of kayaks, but nobody here seemed to believe in the merits of people in small boats. Too inefficient when a motorboat could cover twice as much distance in half the time. Too dangerous, when there were bears and whales and huge swells. I wondered about this, but it was time to shelve the thought of kayaks. My phone rang;

the gruff voice of a bear hunting guide was on the other end. Who was this? he wanted to know. Where was the former permit administrator? Someone new, again? Anyway, he went on, there was another guide's boat anchored in "his" bay. This was unacceptable. What was I going to do about it?

I looked at the map again. The bay he mentioned was enormous, opening like a giant mouth the farther back you went. Two boats were too many? How could I judge that from this office, sitting at a computer? I realized I would need to see this for myself.

"If you can get out here, I'll show you," the guide went on, the tone of his voice implying that he doubted this would ever happen. "But you'd better do something about it," he added. "You're the one who permits these people; you need to manage them better. This bay is mine. It's always been mine."

Tom rolled his eyes, overhearing. He had obviously been in conversations like this before.

Hanging up the phone, I went out back of the storage sheds where the kayaks lay upturned, a gentle carpet of moss covering their hulls. I turned one over and sat inside, uncaring that dampness crept into my jeans. Kayaks could worm their way into the secret places. They could carry a troubled woman far into the solace of a deserted bay. This was how I would also slide my way into the heart of Southeast Alaska. It would be easy. The inner voice would vanish at last. This would be the place where I was good enough. This, the place I would stay.

two

There were so many things I didn't know: how to drive the skiff, how to tie a bowline knot, how to face up to the guides who paced in their rubber boots, demanding what I knew about bears anyway. Their piercing, hooded eyes beamed right through me and summed me up: outsider. Won't last long.

I was trying to find home the only way I knew how. I had bought a house, joined a gym. Wasn't that what people did? But Alaska hid in scraps of cloud, in the soft rain that seemed to leak from the sky, in the threatening sea. Like me, Alaska was hard to know. An unwelcome suitor, I tagged behind it, tugging on its sleeve.

Now I was on a small slice of beach somewhere on Chichagof Island, burning down an outlaw cabin. We had pulled out all the unburnable plastic and the items that someone might want back, though nobody ever appeared at the office to claim those things, knowing that a hefty ticket awaited them. Sven had liberally doused the plywood walls with gasoline and thrown a match. The cabin went up in a fireball that threatened to torch the trees nearby.

The three of us crouched on the sand, waiting for the roof to cave in. Mandy, the woman tasked with recording and planning for these cabins' destruction, was still chuckling over my inept piloting at the skiff's tiller. I had spun the boat in circles instead of driving true, and she didn't understand why I couldn't master such a simple task. Every so often she waded out and pushed the boat back so it floated free. She knew how to do everything, and in contrast I felt like a complete beginner.

Boats were the tools everyone used on the arteries around the islands, and there was a delicate balance to maneuvering through the shoals that ran dry at low tide, and angling to avoid a face full of cold spray. The maps were incomprehensible lines with depths listed in fathoms. The whole place was like a foreign language and I doubted I would ever learn it. I looked over my shoulder, imagining the bears stacked up in the woods, waiting to pounce. This country was getting the best of me.

Boredom finally got to Sven. "Shake shake shake, shake your booty," he sang off-key, dancing down the beach. Singing was part fun and part necessity: it could pass the time but also alert bears to our presence. Perpetually cheerful, Sven sang constantly, oblivious to the fact that he could not carry a tune.

Trying to ignore the knot of fear in my stomach, a sour stew consisting of bears and the ocean and my inadequacy, I poked through the driftwood flung knee high on the beach, hoping for a fishing float, those translucent blue glass balls that Japanese fishermen used to attach to their nets before relinquishing to plastic. I had never seen one, but Sven could walk right by the same spot and scoop one up. He had the eye, he said. I was unlucky again. My search turned up only a handful of plastic bottles, recently adrift from across the ocean.

A bear hunting boat steamed slowly by, its occupants flourishing binoculars in our direction. We would hear about this later, in town. To some locals, this was a classic case of federal overreach—burning down cabins that, in their eyes, were on public land and therefore allowed. What was wrong with a simple plywood shack in all those acres of land?

These outlaw cabins were built by the dauntless and the intrepid, the guys we saw heading out to sea with lumber piled high in a small skiff. The cabin builders always picked the secret hideaways they thought we would never find: bays drained dry at low tide, peppered with saw-toothed rocks that could gouge a prop faster than you could react. They hauled windows, generators, and kitchen sinks and got to work. Sometimes they covered the roofs with camouflage netting so they could not be seen from the air, Sven had told me. The cabins were a dare to us, the feds. Find us if you can.

They never actually lived in the cabins; these were meant to be retreats. They were the escape routes from town when it all got to be too much: the wife, the kids, the routine. We never saw anyone at the cabins. The owners knew better—a ticket would have come their way, perhaps a mandatory court appearance. Besides, everyone knew where we were and when we would be there. The cabin builders talked to each other on their secret radio channels. They watched us as we pulled out of the harbor and noted what direction we took. They knew when to make themselves scarce.

For every fancy cabin, there were more unkempt messes. Most of the cabins we found were barely worthy of the name: sheets of Visqueen nailed to suffering trees, and that was it. Rings of litter surrounded the area like the moons of Saturn. Coolers chewed by bears, lawn chairs with dubious staying power, cast-off bits of clothing shredded by weather—it all came to rest near the structure. The builders attacked the remaining trees for fire-wood, sawing down anything living or dead. Dubious murky latrines were built only a few paces from water. The scene resembled a desperate hovel.

I stalked the beach, noting the sins of the occupants. Here they had removed bricks from a historic cabin for a fire ring. There, they had desig-nated a trash dump instead of hauling out their trash. A net hung in the trees for no apparent purpose.

In designated wilderness, there were supposed to be no structures besides ones that met the historical artifact criteria, like the miners' cabins built fifty years before. We could not touch those, no matter how trashy they were. Alaska residents could take advantage of a provision nobody else had, where they could get a permit for a tent cabin outside the wilderness for hunting and trapping for several hundred dollars a year, but the outlaws did not want to be beholden to a government permit. They didn't want to pay for a cabin. If they wanted a cabin, they would build it. If we found it, they would build another one. The cabins stretched in a long sneaky line through the islands of the archipelago. It was how people claimed a foothold in this land. I couldn't completely deny that I understood this urge to colonize.

I watched as Sven took a turn wrestling with the skiff, pushing it out into deeper water as the tide receded. He looked unhappy for once. It seemed that we spent a lot of time babysitting those boats. Engines failed at inopportune times, leaving us to call for rescue from the mother ship. Props fouled in the kelp. They ran out of gas, or water infiltrated the fuel. They took on water. The shallowest bays were off limits to us. Plus, I lived in fear of running aground on an uncharted rock. Sven liked to say that there were two kinds of people: those who had hit rocks and those who hadn't yet. I motored slowly, incurring his impatience, imagining the sudden, sickening crunch.

I could tell already that the boat would never come to be second nature to me the way it was to the locals, as familiar as driving a car. If I was going to stay, I would have to find another way to do it. Something nonmotorized, not bullying its way over the water the way the boats did.

I watched Sven stomp back up the beach from moving the boat again. "We have to stay until this fire goes out, and the tide will start going out soon. We'll have to Indian anchor it. If the anchor doesn't hold, you'll have to swim for it," he announced.

I looked with misgiving at the slate-gray sea. I knew he meant it.

Sven had made me drive the skiff from where the ranger boat was anchored, declaring I needed the practice. He perched like an ungainly bird on the bow, hollering orders. "Get it on step!" he yelled. Over the growl of the motor, I gathered what he meant. At a certain speed, "step," the boat performed best. To do this, you added enough speed that the boat's hull rose up out of the water and reduced drag. Any less, and the boat rolled sluggishly or crashed into the chop. Step was fast, though, not much time to react to the passenger's frantic signals.

There was an established ritual to driving a powerboat. The passenger in the bow scanned for rocks and hollered back when the ocean floor rose to a dangerous level. There was skill, too, reading the sea and angling the boat so that everyone aboard was not drenched by rogue waves. As we approached shore, the driver hauled the prop up and all seized oars to push the boat the rest of the way. Once the bow ground to a halt in the gritty sand and pebbles of the beach, we evaluated the tide.

A rising tide was no problem, unless the anchor slipped. Securing the bowline to a log or tree above the expected height, we were free to leave for several hours. Knowing this, we still took the precaution of hauling our float coats, massive orange coats that doubled as life vests, with their pockets full of survival items, well above the tide, just in case. Then when it was time to go, we just reeled in the line hand over hand until the boat floated to us.

A falling tide presented more challenges. We had to return to the boat frequently to ensure we were not left high and dry. With crossed fingers and a prayer, we perched the anchor on the bow and shoved the boat off into the deeper water, yanking the line to drop the anchor once the boat was far out enough. Despite this, the boat sometimes homed back to shore, requiring this tactic over and over again. Plus, the mudflats set up sticky, trapping unwary walkers who misjudged them.

It all seemed like a lot of work, beginning with the uncoupling of the skiff from the mother ship and ending with the return, an uneasy timing of neutral gear to avoid slamming into the ranger boat. The ranger boat captain hustled out of the wheelhouse to watch impassively, arms folded, doubting my skill. Once, holding the skiff to keep it from escaping from the ranger boat while Sven scrambled to tie a bowline, I even fell in the water, necessitating a rescue and drying out. From the safety of the ranger boat, Mandy shook her head and I slunk aboard, dripping cold seawater. I imagined what she was thinking: I would never belong here. I had to find a way to prove her wrong. If motorboats weren't the way, I would find another one.

"We could find a lot more of these cabins with kayaks," I ventured as Sven came dripping back to the fire. Kayaks could move in inches of water. They were silent, not tipping off outlaws the way our skiffs did. And just think, I went on, we could check on the guides without them knowing days in advance as our ranger boat lumbered slowly up the coast, the VHF radio giving notice of our presence long before we arrived. We could monitor the historic sites that the archaeologists never had time to reach. We could pull weeds, a never-ending battle. It would be much cheaper than the ranger boat, which averaged $10,000 an outing. We could do dozens of trips for that, I finished up with a flourish.

The remains of the cabin gave up, the overhead supports we had not been able to remove by hand tumbling to the earth. Now we faced only a pile of burning logs, which would take forever to smolder out. The tide slowly seeped down the beach, the boat in danger once again.

Sven wrinkled his forehead. Why would anyone want a boat without a motor? he wanted to know, but he didn't say no outright. It was true that these ranger boat trips were expensive, and there was a kayak program up the coast on another district that seemed to be a success. A good program here might bring kudos down from the regional office. But I had to have training, he insisted. There was a guy who owned a kayak shop downtown. He gave classes. "Wyatt's his name," Sven said. "Take a class, bring me a certificate, and then we'll see." He shrugged, poking the fire with a stick. "Might as well give it a shot," he said. As long as he didn't have to do anything except sign some training forms, he added. He had enough to do with wrestling the sliver of budget he got, sending progress reports to the bosses upstairs, and the inevitable staff meetings—all things that none of us had thought about when we joined the Forest Service.

A straight shooter, Sven did not mince words or suffer fools gladly. Part of my job was to analyze the effects of proposed projects on the wilderness, determining whether allowing things like additional bear hunts or fish weirs would harm the solitude and naturalness of the area. Once, he returned a draft report I had submitted with the words "This is bullshit" scrawled across it. My earnest idea of a pure, unsullied wilderness did not fit with the gritty reality of a place that had been used by others for centuries. "Alaska is different," the old-timers all said, and they were right.

Though his endorsement of kayak patrols was only lukewarm, I imagined that Sven saw something in me, an enthusiasm that he had lost over the years of escalating paperwork and bureaucracy. I liked that Sven had faith in me, because I was not at all sure I could pull this off. I could think of several reasons why it would not work.

The most obvious was that I was scared of the sea. I had come close to being swept off my feet in a rapidly filling bay in New Zealand; I had floundered in an impossible swimming class in junior high school, my body sinking as I thrashed the water with windmilling arms. I had never learned to swim. Water and I did not get along.

Still, I was drawn to water in a way I could not explain. I understood that the ocean had layers, from the pale blue surface to the deep floor where light could not penetrate. Because I had layers too, I thought I could understand the ocean. Only a few people ever got below my first layers. I protected myself fiercely, the way the ocean did. If there were mysteries in the ocean, I had my own secrets, just as carefully guarded. In that way, I thought, the ocean and I were just alike.

three

I hadn't always been plagued with a critical inner voice, shadowing every move I made. In the cruel halls of junior high school, I had learned that how you presented yourself to the world was subject to scrutiny. In order to survive the packs of girls who roamed freely, seeking weakness, I had to develop a thick outer shell. Inside, the voice berated me for being so shy, so skinny, so imperfect. I strove to prove it wrong. Someday, when I was out of the confines of school, I told myself that I would show it and the rest of the world that I could be stronger, tougher, braver.

In college, my critic assured me that I was not thin enough, not yet. I had to stick to a brutal regime of minimal calories and long-distance runs, pushed to a fast pace. There was no such thing as an easy run, or a day where I could eat whatever I wanted. If I slacked off, ate a cookie, I was fat and undeserving of love. Later, as I began to fight fires and clear trails, all hard and brutal work that I had thought would extinguish any lingering doubts, the voice was more subdued, popping up like a mushroom to suddenly deliver the bad news: there's still something too different about you. I never knew when it would appear and wasn't sure whether everyone else was hounded by their own voice. Nobody seemed to speak of it, so it seemed like it was only me. Only motion kept this voice at bay.

The first time I slid into a fiberglass sea kayak, I knew that this was what I wanted. This boat bore no resemblance to the sturdy plastic or rubber-bottomed crafts I had paddled on inland lakes and along Florida's mild Gulf. This boat was made to be part of the ocean, not separate. I wanted that too, to be part of Alaska, although the state was doing its best to convince me otherwise.

A small, colorful armada floated just offshore of Silver Bay: Wyatt the kayak instructor and the rest of the students. They waited for me to launch. I had an audience, and all of my paddling in the tropics in a folding boat could not help me now. There, if you fell in on launch, you could laugh and pretend that you meant it. You could float for a few minutes in water as warm as air before trying again.

What are you even thinking? the voice in my head taunted. *What if you fall in and can't get back in your boat? You can't swim! What if you drown?*

I couldn't stand there forever. I gently pushed the boat as far out as I dared, far enough that it floated but not so far that the water would overtop my rubber boots. Standing parallel to the kayak, I laid my paddle across the back deck as a temporary outrigger and, holding on, gracelessly lowered myself into the seat.

The water was sluggish, the slack tide piling up on the beach. The rest of the class watched as I settled myself into the seat, the boat wobbling with a disturbing intensity. The kayak settled deep with my weight and I had to push with my paddle, wincing as the fiberglass scraped the rocks below the surface.

Once I was underway, things were better. My first tentative strokes gave way to smoother ones. I committed to the paddle.

≈

"You need a boat," the locals had said. They recognized island fever when they saw it. Everyone had boats, shaggy-haired teenagers piloting family Lunds through the channel before they were legally able to drive, snout-nosed fishing boats for catching the daily limit, any kind of boat that ran. Sometimes, they told me, you just needed to get off the island. Gain perspective. It was the only way, they said, to survive.

They all owned powerboats of various sizes, capable of buzzing over to Kruzof Island in less than an hour. Some of the boats barely floated, low bellied in the water, belching out noxious fumes. Others were fancy drop-bows, sporting two motors and bristling with fishing rods. They shared space with the working boats, the trollers and seiners and scows. Everyone, it seemed, had a means of escape.

Though I had brought it along, my folding boat would not cut it here. Meant for flatwater, it had a rubber bottom that radiated the temperature beneath. It had no spray skirt. I needed something beefier than that.

My new kayak came wrapped in layers of padding, loaded onto a barge in Seattle and shipped the slow way north. When I cut through the bubble wrap, I caught my breath as I looked at its sleek design and sunshine color. This was a brave boat, meant to cut through lumpy seas. It was not the fastest boat around, measuring a wide twenty-four inches across the beam, but it was a compromise between stable and fast. It stayed true to a heading and slid through water like a knife through hot butter. This, I thought, was my ticket to the ocean. This, an escape route if I needed it.

≈

Although it wasn't reciprocal, I was falling in love with this new country. It was true: Alaska was different, starting with the climate. Beginning as the Black, or Kuroshio, Current near Japan and later splitting off as drift from the main current, this moderating force swept past the archipelago, keeping water temperatures at a relatively balmy forty-two degrees and ensuring a maritime climate, with little variation in summer and winter temperatures. Clouds covered the sky 80 percent of the time in a normal year. The result of this was like living beneath a pane of fogged glass nearly all the time.

The women who had lived here for decades looked younger than the calendar said, untouched by the sun's damaging rays. I hoped that this boon would be retroactive, erasing the fine lines that spread like fans from beside my eyes. My formerly straight hair sprang into soft curls. Sometimes I thought that I was unrecognizable from the woman I had once been.

My wardrobe changed too. Gone were soft cotton and denim. Instead, I rotated between layers of polypropylene and wool, topped by whatever rainwear was appropriate for the occasion. There was the town raincoat, suitable for dashes between the house and office; the hiking waterproof, a tougher cousin; and finally, the all-day deluge wear—full-on rubberized pants held up by suspenders and overlain by a nonbreathable coat that kept sweat in as much as it kept rain out. Everything revolved around keeping dry.

I had opened the back of my truck one day to find a lacy green mold covering the black heels I had ambitiously brought from the mainland. There was nowhere to wear such fanciful shoes anyway. It didn't matter how far I was walking, I almost always wore XTRATUFs, the ubiquitous rubber boots that people nicknamed Sitka Sneakers. I wore them with jeans, rain pants, and dresses. Floppy and without arch support, they were terrible for my feet but were the best footwear for a place that saw more than one hundred inches of rain a year. I bought a boot dryer and a dehumidifier, trying to combat the eternal damp.

The language was even different here, peppered with local sayings. "Where's your wife?" Sven would holler as we motored past a fishing boat. The man at the wheel leaned out his window.

"Left her on the beach!" he yelled back.

At first, I scanned the unforgiving shore, looking for the tiny dot that would signify a person, but then I learned that this meant that his wife had stayed home. Even the term "beach" was misleading. I had spent seven seasons in Florida, and there a beach meant sand so hot you sprinted across it barefoot, the occasional palm tree to lie under, and water that you could float in for hours, suspended on a layer of salt.

Not so in Southeast Alaska. Here, a beach could range from a wedge of hard-packed grit to a cobble-strewn landing, worried by surf.

In town, if someone was going to travel to the dead end that marked the boundary of where you could drive, they were "going out the road." If someone was getting on a plane to leave Alaska for the Lower 48, they were "going to America."

They stood outside in the rain, chatting it up, seeming not to notice the fine mist that soaked the shoulders of their wool coats. Here, nobody carried umbrellas. Those were for tourists. Rain was a companion they knew, the sun celebrated but also not to be trusted, an elusive courtesan that left way too soon. Some people even preferred the rain over the sun. "It's way too dry," Sven grumbled, out of sorts after a week without moisture. "We need some rain."

≈

In the mornings, running for the plane that would take me to another island, I had to stop and watch the life that churned above and below the sea.

Rafts of adolescent marbled murrelets, birds that spent most of their lives on the ocean, used their short, stubby wings to fly underwater below the high bridge to the island that held the airport. Bald eagles sat stair-stepped on the limbs of spruce trees, the boughs bending under their considerable weight. Sea lions stalked the fishermen on the cleaning dock, snatching up offal discarded below. The commercial jet's path took me across Baranof Island, interior lakes shining and ice covered far below, a sea of impenetrable mountains, and bays as deep as canyons. So much wild land, places where nobody had ever walked. Pressed against the airplane window, bracketed by tourists on the other three sides, I was overcome with this country's immensity.

Right after I had moved to Alaska, the friend of a friend had called to invite me to his island. I hesitated: I barely knew him. We had met back in Idaho on a brief weekend outing, accompanied by our mutual friend. The three of us had spent the day before the New Year skiing in below-zero temperatures to a remote cabin. He had been funny and interesting, though when I passed him on skis, climbing a hill, he had appeared annoyed that he could not stay ahead and had charged on once we reached the flats, leaving me behind in the bitter cold as he raced to the cabin.

I held the phone, thinking. In the past, I had done brave things: hitchhike through New Zealand, march into burning forests, drive cross-country solo. At the same time, I had closed up my heart like a drawstring, avoiding fear and heartbreak. I thought of the lonely husbands. I thought of the map in my head, all the places I had lived, crisscrossing the country like fine threads. Hadn't I said I wanted to stop? "I'll come," I said.

To get to his house, I had to board a plane, disembark in another coastal town, and then endure a slow ferry or take my chances on a floatplane filled with other passengers vomiting quietly into airsick bags. But when I stepped onto the dock, he was there, huddled against the rain in an orange fleece jacket, his eyes the color of the sea. A jolt of possibility, as unexpected as lightning, sizzled through my skin. What would it be like, I thought then, to really be known? How did I even start? I had let nobody into my heart for years, instead cultivating the tough outer skin I showed everyone. Suddenly, as I watched this man hoist my bag into his pickup, saw his casual grin, this seemed like no way to live.

I added up all the casualties I had left behind: perfectly good men, all of them, sacrifices to a life I had spent moving across the country in search of the next, better place. I thought of the men who had left me, too, their last bitter words echoing in my ears. I was too independent, didn't need them, would never change. I thought I had missed my chance, that it was too late. Maybe I had been wrong. This, the last place I would ever live. This, the last man I might ever find.

≈

Falling in love in Alaska was not like falling in love anywhere else. Here the immediacy of life and death was right in my face. The fishermen who never came home, the planes that never returned; all of these events made me believe that I had to make a leap of faith, because life here could be cut short instantly. One day I flew back from Juneau in a whiteout, the plane wrapped in fog so thick that the pilot ascended and descended to find clear air, white-knuckling it home. At the float dock, we exchanged a brief glance, knowing we had been lucky.

A relationship that is long distance, two people on different parts of the same ocean, can be like the fog, hiding things that matter. The same as the pilot peering through an obscured sky, I spiraled up and down, trying to keep our connection alive. I punched through the silence that punctuated our phone calls; he just wasn't the talkative sort, I deduced. Seeing him only once every few weeks, I forgot what I had begun to suspect: people were like the ocean, made up of layers that could be known only over time. I saw the sunlit surface, and after years of being alone, that was enough. In the short days we had together, he sparkled; he was the ocean's top layer.

I had seen little sparkle in the grim town where I had recently lived. Most people were too focused on survival to shine. They pushed forward relentlessly against a stark landscape that wanted to flood, burn, or starve them out. There, smiles were hard won. Frivolity was not encouraged.

I thought that I too had lost my former sparkle. I remembered Finn asking what had happened to me. I wanted to reclaim the girl I used to be, the one who had enough sparkle for the entire night. That we never talked about anything substantial in my new relationship, I forced out of my head. There would be plenty of time for that later. Because we had so few hours together, now was the time to forget the lonely years. Now was the time to have fun. Somehow we never got around to anything but skimming the surface. This seemed like enough.

For two years I made this journey between islands, each of us living our separate lives in long absences. In the past, I had never loved anyone long distance; a clean break had seemed the best approach.

But that was the way of things here. Fishermen left their wives for weeks at a time. The bear hunting guides often had winter families in other towns, never seeing them all season until the hunts were done. In this little town, huddled with mountains at our back and ocean in front, crowded into the scarce space that nature gave us, people paired up, split apart, and paired up again. The only constant was people together. Solo individuals swam against the current in a place where shoulders were needed, talismans against everything that could go wrong. I wanted to have what they had.

On his island, we went for walks, long strolls on afternoons when the wind kept us tethered to shore. The island he lived on had been under attack in the past, viciously razored of old-growth trees. Like an old woman, it still retained a suggestion of its former beauty as we climbed above the remaining tree line to alpine tundra. In the distance the ocean rolled in a long, slow swell.

"I hope you always hold my hand," he said then in a rare moment of emotion. After all the seasons of leaving men behind or having them leave me, I thought, maybe I had found one I could stay with, and one who would stay with me.

After years of elusiveness, it was time, I told myself, to stick. To grow up, to stop looking for something better. Maybe there was nothing better. There were other women jetting all over the state just like me with a backpack and hope, and I wanted to be out of that club.

Here in Alaska, we were pinned down by more than just gales. All sorts of things conspired against a person here: the eternal winter darkness, the inability to escape. In my first year, Tom took off, seeking a city where his kids could have more opportunities. Other families left too. Kids went off to college and never came back, lured by the sun to settle elsewhere. Here you could feel locked between the mountains and the water. Your choices could seem very narrow, just like the small slice of land on which you had claimed a stake.

After all, I was replaceable. The men I had left behind had waited barely long enough for the dust from my truck tires to flatten in the mountain air before finding some other girl. Maybe this man would work out when the others had not. I convinced myself it would be easy, a long, slow paddle on a helpful sea.

paddler's box

The paddler's box is an imaginary boundary. Draw a rectangle over your shoulders, past your arms, to where you hold the paddle in front of you. Now tell yourself that wherever you move in the boat—because you must move with the boat, not sit in it like you are fashioned of wood—you will keep your upper body within that box.

At first, the paddler's box will feel confining. You will forget and stray outside the lines. You will do what comes easier, drawing on your arms to propel you instead. That's not how it works. In the box, you learn to use everything you have to give. In that way, you and your boat become one, not fiberglass and blood, not separate, but one complete being.

one

"Stay in the paddler's box!" Wyatt yelled, studying me carefully. The water was slow today, without the push of wind to help out. Our boats were the color of sun, the only brightness in a world that had suddenly gone steel gray.

The other students turned in lazy circles, practicing all the strokes: the scull, the ferry, the back paddle. With town and land blotted out, the entire landscape was our canvas to mark up however we wanted. Everything was gone: the hulks of the cruise ships anchored in the sound, the cigar-shaped lighter boats ferrying tourists to town and back, even the lives we led in town. The fog had eaten it all.

The breath of the fog was a clammy kiss on my cheek. We had seen it coming, a rolling tide swallowing up the outer islands, and now we were completely embraced by it. We could have been a mile from shore, or two hundred. In the fog, we could have been anywhere.

The muffled thump of a bell in the buoy tower nearby told me we were somewhere near the Eastern Channel, the place that laid us wide open to the sea, but this encompassed a whole sweep of ocean, from the tideflats to the outer reaches of Silver Bay. I imagined us paddling in circles forever, but Wyatt directed us to focus on our compasses and charts to find our way back home. This was dead reckoning, he told us. You had to trust yourself and your instruments, even when it seemed that you were heading the wrong way, out to sea.

We were all bad at the paddler's box. New kayakers flung themselves with enthusiasm all over their boats, windmilling their arms in an attempt to move forward. But if you went outside the lines of the box, you wouldn't last long. Your arms would give out before your heart did. Kayaking was all about finding the smooth way, the easier way.

The paddler's box, Wyatt explained, holding the side of my boat as we rafted up together, meant that you could trace an imaginary line from your hands to your shoulders. But you didn't just stay in one place, facing forward. The paddler's box was fluid: it moved with you as you rotated. It wasn't static; it adapted to the waves and tide. You moved your torso as you adjusted to what was coming at you, Wyatt lectured, not your arms. It was flow, not force. You didn't fight the water. You moved with it instead. He grinned, mist painting his hair silver under his ratty ball cap. "Make sense?" he asked.

I nodded my head, trying to understand. Even on calm days like this one, the ocean was still a muscle, currents and tide combining to an insistent shove under my boat. I had always thought that the right way was to be stronger than the water.

I had always forced my way through things, asserting my right to be there in a world that didn't always want me around. On the fire crew, brute force mattered. We hauled forty-pound water containers in each hand, chainsaws tipped over our shoulders. We pushed our way through twenty-four hours without sleep, pulling ash-smeared hoses that snarled and tangled in head-high brush. On the trail crew, we blasted tread out of rock, tamping down loose dirt with steel rock bars that jarred our fore-arms with every movement. We dug with Pulaskis into stubborn hillsides, building switchbacks. There wasn't any other way to do it, I had been told. I had been aware of being part of a sisterhood; the few women who could, or wanted to, do this kind of work. You didn't let the sisterhood down by showing weakness. We had worked too hard to break into places that men thought should belong only to them.

I had spent hours trying to become strong, because that was prized above all else. That worked for some things, but not for kayaking. For kay-aking, I was trying too hard.

At first the paddler's box felt confining, a prescribed way to paddle. Why couldn't I just do what I wanted, drag a paddle through the water in my own way? I didn't want to think about it. I wanted to just do it, the way I had always done things: throw myself into it with everything I had, lungs burning, sweat like rain on my skin. No thought of consequences, just full speed ahead. Redlining was second nature, that push to the absolute edge. But the more I tried it, staying in the paddler's box, the more I fell into an uncomplicated circle, arms rising and falling, paddle skimming the water instead of pushing it. My boat leaped forward with no effort, a thin wake foaming behind me. I was going so fast, faster than I had ever gone before.

"You shouldn't clench the paddle in a death grip, either," Wyatt said, observing the way my neoprene gloves choked up on the handle. He exe-cuted a seamless circle around my boat, showing me. You should be able to lift your fingers off the paddle if you want and still move forward, he said. "Try it like this." It wasn't force, but acceptance. Once you accepted the water and what it gave you, you were able to move within it. It was as though I were slipping inside the ocean's skin, an ally instead of an opponent.

That was hard for me to believe. A nonswimmer who should have been miles from an ocean, I clutched at my life vest with the fervor of a prayer. Not letting on that I could barely dog paddle, I also didn't reveal that I did not trust the sea. Even on a calm day, it seemed to lie in wait, revolt bub-bling up from under the surface. It seemed that at any time it could turn against me.

But part of me was drawn to the water despite my fear of it. I planned to learn to swim, someday, I told myself. Until then I would fake it, make sure I never capsized. I knew others before me had thought the same thing and come to grief, but on a day as calm as this one, it was easy to convince myself this was the way things would always be.

I had thought paddling would come easy. I had bought my first kayak when I lived deep in the Florida Everglades, working on a firefighting crew. I bought what I could afford and what I could carry. A woman, I thought, should be able to tote her own kayak. That had always been my philosophy, born more of circumstance than of values. Also, the boat could fit in my truck.

It was a boat made of fabric and rubber, composed of myriad confusing and easily lost parts. It took considerable strength to snap the skeleton into the skin. I pieced it together, cursing as mosquitoes hung in dark clouds on the riverbank. Not built for comfort or speed, the boat tortured the back and butt and wobbled uncertainly in wind.

But it got me places. I dragged it down tea-colored rivers, walking when the water got too shallow. I took it onto ponds frequented by alligators, round, sparkling freshwater holes full of small, slippery bream. I even took it out onto the Gulf, dodging motorboats. I thought I knew what I was doing. It was clear that I had survived through a combination of luck and fair seas.

"Time to head back," Wyatt said. We unspooled ourselves from the backstrokes and turns we had been trying out and followed the bearing we had set.

As we moved closer to town, a yellow kayak emerged from the fog, captained by a woman whose hair was the color of flame. I knew her name was Rowan because I had seen her around; she was a solo traveler, like me. Seeing us, she laughed, captivated by our flotilla where moments before she had thought herself all alone. She had been paddling by herself, and I wondered how many other people were out here, completely unseen and unknown. I liked how brave she was, following her own dead reckoning, undeterred by what she could not see. I twisted in my seat to watch her pass before she winked out, gulped up by fog again.

When we approached the concrete ramp that marked the transition from water to land, from what could be to what was, nothing I could see was any different. There was still the arc of cloud-shrouded mountain, the ancient, moss-covered cars parked in rows at the marina. There were still tourists clogging the walkway between library and museum. There was still everything that I couldn't see, the things that dogged me on land but somehow seemed to slip away on the water.

But somehow everything was different. I took a deep breath and balanced my paddle across the back of the cockpit to steady my legs, unaccustomed to standing. With varying degrees of elegance, all of us slid from our boats to the land.

I watched the others as their real lives settled back on them like thick black cloaks. Our grace deserted us as we trudged to our cars with dry bags. There had to be a secret I didn't know, a rule for land just like the ones for the boat, a way to glide through just like the paddler's box, calm and unafraid.

two

The man I would later marry saved my life on a remote and surf-tossed beach. It was not Alaska but Hawaii where I nearly drowned and was rescued from the sea.

We had parked our rental car and hiked through black lava rock to get to this unmarked coastline, on a brief respite from our respective rain-cloaked islands. Large rollers smashed the sand, and I went out only as far as my toes could touch. When the riptide caught me in its invisible grasp, I was hurtled farther out, suddenly unrooted from the land.

I caught his glance from where he stood on the sand, changing from puzzlement to concern. "I can't get back!" I screamed. He and two strangers leaped into action, making a chain that brought me back to shore. It was a gesture I never forgot: disregarding his own safety to rescue me, a hand reaching out across a suddenly hostile sea.

Later, in protected waters, we snorkeled together, our Alaska-white skin glowing under the ocean as if lit from within. We sat on the porch of our vacation house, eating the sweet fruit that hung in orange globes on the trees outside. There was so much fruit that we couldn't eat it all, but I gobbled it up greedily as if I could; it was like eating the sun. We didn't talk about the day I had almost died. He didn't chastise me for my panic in the water, my inability to do what you were supposed to do, swim parallel to the shore until the riptide released its grip. I loved him for that particular silence.

Even still, I almost called off our wedding the day before we married, standing barefoot in front of a white sparkly dress. *I'm not sure about this,* I almost said. *This isn't what I want.* Marriage seemed so final, the slam of a door. I wasn't at all sure I could navigate it.

And there had been signs along the way. Friends looked puzzled, unable to connect the dots of us being together. We were so different, they said. Didn't I worry about that? He did have moods, one friend who had known him longer confided. I had to be sure I could weather those, she said. Was I sure?

They also knew my propensity for moving on. They had weathered years of my changing addresses. Marriage didn't seem to fit with that, they pointed out. How was I going to stick with this, when I hadn't stuck with anything else?

For every night that we hiked out with his telescope to gaze at rare stars, shoulders touching as we stared up at the profoundness of the night, there were warning signals that we weren't right together. There were days when we did not seem to mesh, when an unseen cloud pressed down heavy and thick over us, a cloud I could not seem to dispel. When I broke the silence to reveal secrets I had long kept, like the hungry years, there was no answering glance of recognition. There was silence, so much silence.

But everyone was on the way, the wine was ordered, the dinners paid for. In the two years we had been together, we had hiked into the high country to places most people hadn't been. We had run on trails, keeping the same pace. We had been to other countries, kicking our fins alongside ancient, moss-backed turtles. We had even paddled kayaks together, short sit-on-top boats that wouldn't last in the sea but were good enough if you hugged the shore.

Of course, we hadn't really been together. We had lived far apart, never in the same town. He didn't see how I wavered between fear and confidence: Were there bears outside the tent? Should I charge outside and check, or huddle with held breath? Should I paddle today, or wait out the twenty-knot winds? He didn't see the burden of worry I carried with me: Was I doing the right thing? How did I know for sure? He didn't see the deep, molten need to be heard and to be known after years of traveling solo.

There were no charts for marriage, although perhaps, like the marine charts we carried in our boats, it was more like land than sea, a largely blank space that we would have to learn to fill in. The charts had only suggestions of what you might find after you left your boat. It was up to you to ground truth it.

I had avoided marriage and commitment before like a feral creature, and it had left me here, forty years old and alone. I was tired of the pitying glances from friends and strangers, the undercurrent nobody brought themselves to speak: *You're how old? And you're still single? What's wrong with you?* It seemed like the world swam in pairs; that was the natural way. Women of my age who were single were thought to be in limbo; surely this couldn't be what they had intended. Though I told myself I didn't care what others thought, a part of me believed them. There had to be some reason I was still alone.

This is what you wanted, I told myself fiercely. *You wanted a home, and this is part of that home. You can't back out now.* I thought of the trail of men I had left behind, all the reasons I had given myself to go and not stay. Among my friends, I even had a certain level of infamy for this, the one who could never be caught. I was the one who left, the one who could not be trusted with a heart. I wasn't that person anymore, I told myself, slipping shiny fabric over my head. I had left that woman behind.

≈

After the wedding, my husband moved to my island to a job he didn't really want but took for my sake. He took over the rooms that had been mine. He had so much stuff, way more than I did, boxes that hadn't been opened since his last move and that he had no plans to open now. I realized that I didn't know how to share. Even in boats, I had always preferred paddling solo. It was something else I was going to have to learn.

The marriage soon closed in, a steel trap, snapping shut. Alaska closed in too, huge seas keeping me on the beach, fog dogging my footsteps. Neither love nor country was what I had expected.

After all, there were plenty of men in Alaska. The fishermen sat in hooded sweatshirts grimy with fish guts in an unchanging row in the bar, smoke settling like a second skin on their hopeful faces. The bear hunting guides steamed in on their aluminum boats, long-legged, war-scarred men who taught me how to shoot a .375 rifle. The cannery workers lived in the woods, setting up elaborate tent camps just off the trails. They skied the steeps, postcollege kids in search of a dream, willing to do anything, even work the cannery slime line to stay here for a season or two. I could have chosen any of them, but I hadn't. I had chosen this one, and it was up to me to make it work.

Alaska was completely different than I had expected too. First, there were many different types of rain, and what you wore in each kind mattered. There was the right way to hang up a kitchen tarp to keep off the rain while you cooked at camp. You needed to know how to read aerial photos so you could find the muskeg and stay out of the brushy cedar. You had to know the tide cycle and where the rocks lurked and how to avoid the shipping lanes.

You had to be able to unzip the sticky zipper on your dry suit when you had to pee. You had to stay away from the slippery green slime or you would go down face first on the rocks. Alaska was not a place to escape the person you did not want to be. I was learning this like I was learning paddle strokes—the slow and elegant scull, the sprightly ferry stroke, the brace that could save my life.

Learning my husband was not coming easy. I had thought I had known him, but there were many more layers than I had ever suspected. There were days when I thought he did not want me to know him at all. On those days he would vanish to the gun range, a place where men were taciturn and solemn and did not want to know his feelings. He would turn the television up loud, anything to keep from speaking.

Then he would surprise me with a quirky gift: multicolored plastic spatulas arranged like a bouquet, a certificate I had won for an essay framed and hung on the wall. I was always off balance, never knowing which man would greet me at the door: the one who sparkled or the one who had lost his flame. *Yes*, I would think. And then, *no*. Maybe this was what love was like, I thought. After all, my track record wasn't arrow straight.

"You aren't really committed to the marriage if we don't merge our bank accounts," my husband said.

It was a simple request, one that was reasonable to make. But I remembered what it had been like to be a seasonal worker, living on boxes of macaroni and cheese, three for a dollar. Crawling under my truck to puzzle out a balky carb because I couldn't afford the mechanic. Every cent I had saved had been through the hardest work I had ever done: on the fireline twenty-four hours straight, on the trail carrying seventy pounds on my back.

This was my own fault, I knew. There had been so many things we had not discussed. We had lived on our separate islands all the years we had known each other. Now, on the same piece of ground at last, we were beginning to see the truth of who we really were.

Maybe I was being selfish, I thought. In marriage, you were supposed to share everything, even the scraps of money you had managed to hang on to in years of moving. He was right: merging was not something I understood. I thought of the places where freshwater dumped into the ocean, how the two strands of water kept themselves briefly separate. One finally capitulated and was absorbed into the other. There was probably a lesson to be learned from that.

I went to the bank. I tried to merge our lives. It would be like tying a bowline knot, I thought. I had struggled with this simple knot for weeks, carrying a piece of rope with me everywhere.

"If you can't tie knots, tie a lot," Sven had teased, as I sat with lines spilling over my lap. "Pass the end of the rope," I muttered, fumbling with fingers that felt too thick. When I finally got it, the result looked too simple to hold a boat to a mooring. Surely it needed something stronger, something flashier. But the bowline worked, and, I hoped, braiding our lives together would too. We would just need to practice, the way I had puzzled over the knot until it finally, magically, had worked. Now I could tie a bowline without even thinking about it. If I thought too much about it, I couldn't remember the steps, but if I let my fingers take over, the knot came easy. A heart could be like that too, remembering what the mind forgot.

three

There were days that I thought I was falling out of love with my husband.

The days that I thought this I lifted my kayak off the ground behind our house and placed it on the wheeled cart. The kayak weighed fifty-eight pounds and was over seventeen feet long and I had to center it correctly in the cart or it would bang its delicate fiberglass skin on the pavement or the beach cobble. I had done this once already, a chunk falling out of the bow because I was careless, because I was impatient.

The kayak I bought for my husband hung on the wall outside the house, unused, a thin skin of moss covering it like fur. He had used it once, twice maybe. It had cost $2,000. The first time we went paddling together he swamped the boat close to shore, getting in wrong. He cursed and stomped along the beach while I floated in the bay. Onlookers turned their faces. It was a small town, after all.

I walked down the street pulling my cart, past the kids worrying a storm drain, past the questionable apartments where the police always stopped, pausing at the two lane, sprinting across, going down the dirt access road to the beach.

My husband, sitting on the couch watching colorful players chase a ball across a field, watched me go down the street without curiosity or desire. He did not help me lift the boat or tie it to the cart. He did not want to go along. He wanted to be left alone.

I remembered when it had been different. He had asked me to marry him on the second day of a goat hunting trip. We had been dropped off by floatplane at a lake far above tree line. A gale came in that night and lashed our tents. A bear walked by sometime after midnight, close enough to touch.

Somehow, being asked in this way, in this unusual place where the tundra was turning yellow and gold, seemed like an omen. Surely this must be the right person, I thought. I did not realize at the time that he was the only one of us who wanted to kill a goat, an animal he would not eat but would place on the wall. When we did see a goat, I held my breath and let it out slowly when I saw it was a group of nannies.

I ferried my gear to the low tide line. The water sparkled and I checked the trees for wind. At my house a developer had cut all the trees that I used to use as a gauge for determining whether it was safe out in the Eastern Channel. Now I found that I was fooled half the time, paddling out only to discover a sneaky east wind, whipping up the swell.

Today it looked OK. I stowed the paddle float between the bungee cords that crossed my bow. Remembering Wyatt's admonition to keep a clean deck, I put a water bottle and jacket behind my seat instead of lashing them on top. I ran back to the bushes where the tide would not reach and hid the kayak cart deep inside. Then I pulled the straps of my spray skirt over my shoulders and shrugged on the yellow life vest. My kayak was yellow too. It had to be. Out here you had to be seen. Fog came so fast. In a small boat, you were so close to the water.

On the goat hunting trip, we climbed to the ridge, leaving our camp set up, taking a minimum of gear for the day. I had just bought a GPS and I took a waypoint where we would drop off the ridge while my husband waited impatiently, telling me to hurry. As we walked between two valleys, the fog drifted in, closing us in its embrace. Both of us stumbled, lost, disoriented, succumbing to hypothermia in the slanting rain. I remembered my GPS point and turned in the opposite direction of what felt right. We followed the flickering screen safely back.

At our camp, I looked up at the high rock walls that towered over the lake. There was only one way up to the ridge and only one way down. Years before, two men, lost in the fog, had taken out a rope and tried to rappel. The rope was too short. Poking around, I found one of their sleeping bags washed up onshore, tattered and chewed by bears.

I lowered myself into the kayak and flipped down the rudder. There was a moment before the kayak was floating free, when I was suspended between land and sea, when I thought that my marriage might work out. That if only I became a different person, set adrift my expectations, accepted him for who he was, then I wouldn't feel stuck in a box. It almost seemed possible.

Then the tide lifted me out into the water and it was forgotten. There was only the water and the stroke and everything in the seconds between, before each met.

back paddle

Back paddling happens when you are uncertain or just want to buy time. Is that a whale ahead, or just a submerged rock, showing its face at low tide? Is that a bear on the beach where you have planned to camp? Back paddling gives you a chance to reassess. You can't always go forward. There are times to be prudent. There are times to go full stop.

Despite what people think, back paddling is not a sign of weakness. It can be a sign of strength. Here is where you admit all that you do not know.

Disclaimer: this is really called the reverse forward stroke. That is because all you do is dip your paddle in the water and do the opposite of the forward stroke. But let's call it what it really is, shall we?

one

"I've got to get going, the tide's coming in," Jeremiah said. He ran his hand through his close-cropped hair, looking as doubtful as I felt. He was dropping our little trio off forty miles from town and was not expected back for five days. We were the first kayak rangers to travel the Chichagof Island coast. A lot was riding on this trip.

The familiar hum of worry buzzed in my ears. *Where are we going to camp? How are we going to stay dry? You don't know anything about the sea, not this far from town.* We were so far from rescue, alone on this wild coast. In my solo paddles, I had always seen the welcoming arc of town, buildings huddled in a circle around the shore. Worse yet, I had dragged two people along with me, two people who were standing on this same beach waiting for direction.

Jeremiah shifted his feet, wanting to shove off. A heavy belt laden with a gun, Taser, and handcuffs weighed him down, and he looked impatient. He was the law enforcement officer for the forest, tasked with patrolling an impossible stretch of land and sea. He had places to be and couldn't spend all day while I made up my mind.

It was a typical Southeast Alaska summer day, the temperature stuck at about fifty degrees, with the hint of rain that had just been and the rain that was about to come. Linger too long in this weather and you were trifling with hypothermia, hands that refused to work, feet that stumbled. I had seen the effects of this in the people I had tried to save over the years as part of an impromptu search-and-rescue crew. They made bad decisions, abandoned gear, got irrevocably lost. We had to make a move before we ended up like they had.

I could go back right now, I thought. I could make up all sorts of reasons. The weather didn't look good. Too many bears. Something crucial forgotten.

Grit, I thought. I knew I had it, deep down somewhere. I had lost it for a time, but surely I could summon it back. I had tried the ranger boat trips, but it wasn't enough. The growl of our motors assaulted the quiet bays. Sleeping on the boat, we were isolated from the land. Every step we took away from shore wasn't enough to see everything. We were dependent on the tide, always running to free our boats. Once we had misjudged the low tide severely enough that we had labored to haul driftwood across a rocky beach to make a ramp, sweating and heaving the dead weight of the Lund across each log until we finally reached the water.

≈

The two near strangers I had enticed to come along on this maiden voyage, Mark and Rowan, stood watching. I knew Rowan from our chance encounters on the water. We often passed each other in our separate boats, and I had been working up the courage to ask her to paddle together. There weren't many women who paddled alone. She was an independent spirit, unruffled and calm in the face of thick fog or steep waves. She seemed to know everything about kayaks but had never been able to venture so far from town as we were today. This would be unknown territory for us both.

Mark worked on an adjoining district, and I knew him only from laborious meetings where we both tried to stay awake as someone droned on about safety or forest planning. He was hoping to do some kayak monitoring of his own someday, and I had asked him because he, like Rowan, seemed serene in most situations. Going with the flow was something I hoped to absorb from both of them.

"Got everything?" Jeremiah asked. I studied our pile of colorful gear, stuff sacks and extra paddles and life vests and bear canisters, all the things I had gathered to keep us safe. I was sure something was missing; five days seemed like a long time.

Jeremiah thumbed through my set of charts. "I saw a sandy beach a few islands to the south when I was up here before," he said. "See, it's this one." He pointed to a slice of land that looked the same as a hundred others. "Might be a good place to camp."

I studied the land, only a suggestion on the map. Charts were all about the sea, the land not necessary. There wasn't much to indicate what lay there. This was why you took two sets: charts for sea, aerial photos for land. I had seen the beach he was talking about on my aerial photo. Sandy beaches stuck out on the photos, but since the pictures were taken by a low-flying plane, sometimes decades earlier, it was impossible to know how much had changed. The timber crew used photos for marking sale units, and they had told me that they would head confidently for a clearing only to discover it was becoming choked with trees. Could I even find this beach? Was it even still there?

The beach we were on would be a poor camp. Alders crowded the shoreline like crooked teeth. The cobbles we stood on sloped to the sea and would be swallowed up in the high tide.

I gazed past the boat to where the last island met the force of the sea. There was nothing out there but open ocean, and though it looked calm today, I was glad we were heading into the island chain. "I guess we're all set," I said, although I was far from sure.

"Well, see you Thursday," Jeremiah said. He hauled up the drop-bow ramp and secured it with a chain. Ducking inside the cabin, he slowly backed out to sea. A series of small waves from the wake splashed onto the beach, just shy of our feet. The deep chug of the motor was a heartbeat slowly fading. We were on our own, forty miles from town.

I surveyed the pile of gear and the three boats. It seemed impossible that everything would fit inside the hatches. I had packed everything in large dry bags, too large now, I realized.

"I usually put everything in really small bags," Rowan said tactfully, eyeing the pile. I realized she was right. My inner critic piped up. *That was really stupid. They must think you're a complete idiot.* Packing a kayak was like putting together a puzzle. You chose slim dry bags that would slide easily into the crevices of the hatches. You paired these with tiny stuff sacks that could be manipulated into the pockets of air that remained. The heavier items you kept close to the cockpit, lighter things farther out.

Essentials were strapped to the boat or stuffed near the seat: maps in a waterproof case tucked under the bungee cords in front of the cockpit, a water bottle fastened inside, a flat dry bag under the maps with trail mix for long crossings, a fleece jacket under the butt for a cushion. In the middle of the ocean, you didn't want to be jockeying around for an item that was buried deep.

Even though the hatches were supposed to be waterproof, I knew that they could fail. I noticed that Rowan had her sleeping bag in a dry sack and swathed in a garbage bag just in case. She had done the same with her tent. I took mental notes as I poked through the duffels, squeezing air out and trying to reduce their girth. I was used to rain, but only the kind that fell in the mountains. That kind was brief, like stepping into a shower. The sun always came back out, and we rangers had learned to dash for it, spreading our gear over trees to dry. In the Rockies, it had often taken only minutes if you had the right trifecta: wind, sunshine, and a good set of drying trees or boulders. Here, I realized, if you got something wet it stayed that way.

There was nowhere for the large dry bags to fit except strapped to our decks. Wyatt's voice echoed in my head. "Keep a clean deck," he had always said, eyeing the way I had fastened a water bottle onto mine for easy access. What if you had to do a self-rescue? With a bunch of stuff in the way, you would be flailing in a chaotic sea. That had been just a water bottle. What would he say now? As we gingerly crawled into our cockpits, I realized that one big wave could swamp us.

I swiveled my gaze back and forth between Mark and Rowan, trying to gauge their expressions as they paddled their overloaded boats into the narrow channel. I had roughed out an itinerary I thought would work.

Survey for weeds such as reed canary grass or Russian knapweed and GPS their locations so that a crew could come back and treat them. Mark down and assess any campsites on our maps so we could see in later years whether their boundaries were expanding. Check the historic properties in another bay for the archaeologists to ensure they weren't being vandalized. Search for outlaw cabins. Watch for any of my outfitter-guides and make sure they were in the places they were supposed to be. It was a solid itinerary, and Sven had signed off on it, a half grin on his face that said he wasn't quite sure about this endeavor but hoped I would pull it off. Despite his gruff exterior, I had grown fond of Sven and didn't want to disappoint him.

I knew everything about the mountains in the Lower 48—how to cross talus slopes with big slouching strides, my feet sinking deep into pebbles the size of cereal. I knew how to cross rivers, shuffling my feet along the slippery bottom, moving upstream past the point where I wanted to exit. I knew how to crouch low on an inflatable pad as thunderstorms pounded the saddle, swaying slightly on two feet because that was less exposure. I had dodged cranky range bulls, listened to a mountain lion's growls as it stalked my camp, and found my way through July snowstorms. But I didn't know the ocean. My few brief forays onto it, just shy of town, hadn't been nearly enough. But I had learned the mountains, and I could learn the sea. *Grit*, I thought. Day by day I would become a stronger woman, a confident one, the knowledge of this place absorbing into my bones.

We paddled through the maze of islands searching for a campsite. It had taken us so long to load the boats, night would be falling soon. The rain, just a tease back on the beach, got more serious. Every take-out was rocky and steep, the shoreline impenetrable.

The charts were a confusing mixture of annotations I did not understand. What were shoals? I knew the tiny numbers meant fathoms, but I couldn't remember what a fathom was. What was a knot? I didn't know that either, but I was sure we weren't paddling at even one knot, whatever that meant. Our pace was laborious.

The islands depicted on the chart all looked the same. Were we rounding the largest one, or was that in front of us? My fancy black gloves, billed as waterproof back at the store, soaked clear through in seconds.

Spying a likely flat area, I stroked toward an island. "I'll check this one out," I called. Not waiting for an answer, I hurtled myself from my boat. I scrambled ashore, misjudging the water depth. Cold sea trickled over the tops of my boots. I had done it, overtopped my boots, a disaster.

The site was not so promising up close. It was a lumpy mess, patches of skunk cabbage promising a seeping wetness that could broach the undersides of our tents. Fresh piles of bear scat decorated the tall grass.

I wavered in indecision. What if there was nothing else? What if we paddled like this forever, frozen statues in our clumsy boats?

Rowan and Mark waited, floating in their kayaks just offshore. They wore stoic expressions as the rain pelted their jacket hoods. I wondered what they were thinking.

I stood in the rain. My feet would be wet the rest of the trip, with no way to dry them. I had packed thoughtlessly, and I had no idea where I was going. I was overcome with how much there was to know.

"Bears," I hollered, wedging myself back into the boat alongside the rifle. I did not elaborate, hoping that this explanation was enough. Grimly, my companions lifted their paddles and we headed south. In the mountains I had always enjoyed the campsite search. It had been like a treasure hunt, seeking out the perfect view, the softest pine needles. Here, I realized, you were limited by circumstance. Some likely looking areas did not drain, with standing water in pools under the trees. Others were armored with devil's club, tiny thorns embedding into my hands as I pushed through. Still others were inhabited by bears, looking up unconcerned as we paddled past. It was becoming clear that here, you took what you got and called it good.

We paddled for what might have been an hour, or maybe fifteen minutes. With all the weight, my boat felt like a barge, each stroke an effort. I abandoned the paddler's box completely for brute force, digging my paddle in with a savage stroke. The boat wove drunkenly along as I desperately scanned the shore. With every second that passed I imagined a mutiny, my crew wrestling for the satellite phone to call for a rescue.

Then a miracle occurred. We rounded the bottom of an island and a small patch of sand hooked out into the water. Back from that, a stand of deep forest promised a dark but level area for tents. By pure dumb luck, I had found the campsite Jeremiah had suggested.

"Here it is," I called, pretending I had known all along. We shouldered armloads of gear and trudged into the trees, setting up camp with unpracticed effort, except for Rowan, who had her tent up in half the time it took me. As I threw gear around the campsite, I realized I had brought only one tent.

I looked over at Rowan, who was carefully setting out her headlamp and book in her one-person tent. I couldn't ask Mark to share hers. The tent I had brought was allegedly for two people, though it looked barely big enough to fit one. I sighed. "I guess you're bunking with me," I told Mark, who just shrugged; he didn't care.

We cooked a hasty dinner and, without much conversation and by mutual consent, called it a day. I couldn't judge what my partners were thinking as they silently slipped inside the tents.

I lay in my tent, listening to rain plink onto the tarp I had stretched over it and to the echoes of Mark's snores. The ever-present knot of worry I carried with me eased a bit. I had survived the first day on the ocean. Nobody had swamped their boat; we had found a campsite. Maybe, I thought, I could do this. Maybe I could be good at this.

Outside the tent, a few brave Sitka deer roamed, seeking out anything with salt. They crashed through the brush, sounding like an entire army. Mark snored all night with various degrees of tone and volume. At least, I thought, punching my makeshift pillow of fleece clothes, the noise drowned out the sounds of any bears that might be approaching.

≈

"Decaffeinated coffee?" Mark sputtered. He sighed and sat down heavily on a rock. A gentle soul, even he seemed driven to the edge by this revelation. I nodded with guilt. I had lured Mark and Rowan on this trip by promising to take care of all the logistics: boats, gear, and food. I had scurried up and down the aisles of Sea Mart with a monstrously loaded cart, throwing things in with abandon. Somehow, I had picked the wrong coffee. I never drank it, so had not paid attention. What was the big deal? I thought. But apparently, it was a big deal, judging from Mark's slumped posture.

"I'm so sorry!" I beseeched, and Mark just held out a mug with a resigned expression. With each day, he emerged from the tent later and later, but I was too afraid to wake him up, knowing that the withdrawal was brutal. Instead we paddled late into the evenings, the best time to be on the water, I discovered. The evenings were different from the fully charged daytime. They became soft, blurred at the edges, darkness creeping in over the skyline and casting shadows over the beaches we explored. The last to go were the high peaks, a pastel glow lingering as we pulled our boats back onto shore for the night. If there was a soft side to Alaska, this was it.

≈

As we paddled, I studied the chart in the waterproof case in front of me. Slowly I began to read the landscape. This bight with a stream cascading from its belly must be the place marked "waterfall" on the map. This island that fronted the open sea was the one marked "headlands" on the chart. "Ruins" could mean anything, from an old fox farm to an entire village.

I read the water, too, noting the places where the seafloor rose high or dropped abruptly for hundreds of feet. The shallows were where we found forests of bull kelp, which tangled in long sheets between the rocks, trapping all sorts of treasures inside.

In the deeps, I leaned as far over as I dared, peering through layers of blue, the lighter sun-touched water near the surface and all the way down to the unknown currents that flowed deeper than I could dive, even if I were brave enough to dive. Slowly the charts began to make sense, as though I were a child learning to read. I unfurled each one in the morning as Rowan and I waited for Mark to arise, tracing my finger over the route we planned to take. Here, there was freshwater and we could fill up our containers. There, where the chart said "breaks in heavy swell," I had seen the rocks in question, a foaming whirlwind that I knew to steer clear of.

I studied the names, evocative or mysterious: Smooth Channel, protected from open swell by outer islands; Rough Channel, wide open to the sea pouring in from the Outer Rocks. Elbow Passage was exactly like it sounded, an akimbo route opening into a large bay. Three Tree Island contained hundreds of trees. Others, with names hinting of a long-ago past: Kukkan Passage, Tawak Passage. While the land on the charts was still largely a blank slate, there were tantalizing descriptions: "sparsely wooded, numerous swamps and small lakes."

My companions were as captivated as I was. We paddled past a rainbow of color: sea stars splayed on tide-exposed rocks, pink and purple and orange and red. Green anemones clustered on the damp black rocks, fringed like bangs around a face, slowly undulating in the rising water. Herons and eagles competed for space in the sky, and cold breath like smoke marked the passage of slow-moving humpback whales. We saw nobody, and nobody saw us. It felt like we were castaways in a strange and magical land.

On land, we tramped through old canneries, taking notes of what remained: mute posts of docks long tumbled into the sea, the remains of a powerhouse near the waterfall that came out of Rust Lake, a thousand feet above. While Rowan walked the shoreline, Mark and I came upon an entire steam-powered winch, taller than I was, squatting untouched as though it had just been used the day before. It was enormous, looming up from the alders like an ancient sea creature, a relic of long-ago logging days. Each night we paddled farther than we had planned, returning to camp with hands wrinkled from salt, our voices hushed in the exquisite stillness.

I scribbled notes in a Rite in the Rain book: here there was a campsite festooned with old tarps and a few weather-beaten lawn chairs. This was one that was obviously used often, so we laid out a tape measure, recording the "barren core": the spot where vegetation was ground down to dirt. We noted the trees, scarred from an ax or nails, and the places where makeshift toilets had been set up. We packed up what we could and left the rest, photographing the site for future patrols. In another place we found daffodils, remnants of former lives at a mine site. Not really weeds, I thought, instead memories.

On one island we found an outlaw cabin, some Visqueen and plywood nailed to trees, a rough-cut counter for dining on, and some lawn chairs. "I never thought these cabins were a bad thing," Rowan said, but now she saw: the island was littered with beer bottles and other detritus from parties; entire trees had been felled for firewood. We hauled the plywood to the beach for burning and rolled up the Visqueen, naturalizing the site as best we could.

I had been right: my feet were wet the entire time, fresh socks quickly absorbing the dampness of the boots' interior. Mark never quite got used to the lack of real coffee. And he snored with abandon, causing me to stare sleeplessly at the tent walls for hours. But somehow those annoyances were only blips on the radar. It was impossible to be upset when we were the luckiest people on earth.

When five days were up, Jeremiah steamed into our camp, ready to take us home. He was buoyant with the success of a usually rough water crossing that had instead been smoothed flat. "How was it?" he exclaimed, but there were no words to describe where we had been and what we had seen. The three of us lined the beach with sullen expressions. None of us wanted to go home.

two

After the wedding, my husband abandoned the things we had done together with no explanation. He no longer wanted to kayak or hike unless those things were associated with a hunt. None of the movies I rented interested him. He narrowed his focus to two things, hunting and guns, subjects that seemed out of my realm of possibility.

My family had been a tight unit of four that moved through the water in canoes, camping on tiny islands. We took nothing from the land except my father's occasional archery-shot deer. We built small twig fires for warmth and recorded the plants we saw on each hike. In contrast, my husband's greatest dream was to go to Africa to "shoot the Big Five." I could think of no reason to shoot an elephant. I wondered why I had not known this before we married. But of course I hadn't known, because I hadn't wanted to ask. Neither of us had wanted to dive too deep; it had felt like a miracle to me to meet someone so late, after a lifetime of failed relationships. What it meant to him I could not be sure. Maybe it was Alaska, after all. This place, with its gale-force winds and indifferent peaks, could make a person cling to someone else in an effort to feel safe.

I had, I realized, been too enthralled with the mountains we climbed and the wild country we moved through to ask any hard questions. Knowing him had been wrapped up in knowing the land we explored. There had been no room for doubt when we struggled to pitch a tent in the rain, no luxury of misgiving as we tried to find our way in the fog.

I would learn him, I thought, the same way I was learning the ocean charts; slowly and with persistence. I tried to find common ground. We went to the range, and I feigned interest in targets and bullets and reloading. My efforts weren't enough. It was an alien and brutal world, thousands of spent shells littering the ground, abandoned boxes riddled with shots tumbling end over end in the weeds that surrounded the range. Men carried large guns back and forth, watching each other's firepower covertly. There were few women. Though I had to shoot for work, it was something I did without enjoyment. I didn't like the glaze that came over him as he stared down the barrel, the disgust at a poorly aimed shot. I didn't like what felt like pointless reloading, aiming, and firing at paper targets.

"Lean forward," my husband sighed. "Lean into it, not away."

I was never doing it right, just like I never loaded the dishwasher right or cut up vegetables correctly. My husband's corrections echoed the voice in my head that said all the same things. I gave up on going, and my husband didn't seem to care. He never asked again.

He had quit drinking abruptly, claiming he was addicted, and this had changed something in him. The man I had first loved evaporated into someone else. He no longer sparkled. Now he plodded through the days under a deep cloud of unhappiness. Nothing I did seemed to make the sun come out. Instead, he replaced the drinking with a deep need to control everything around him; our routines, what words he let come out of his mouth. As I began to tear down my walls, he retreated. I was too messy, too uncontained for his new life.

After my first kayak patrol, I charged back into my marriage with the enthusiasm of the recently converted. I was going to fix it. I was going to make him love me again, no matter what it took. In doing this, I would fall back in love with him. We would go back somehow to the Alaska newcomers we had been, entranced with the country and with each other. Most of all, I would figure out how to retreat from caring about the lack of closeness, the indifference that seemed to spill off his skin in a strange perfume, the shell he wrapped tightly around his heart. I didn't need those things, I told myself. This was life. This was the way it was. I could no longer afford to be the woman who had discarded every landscape, every man that didn't suit her.

Gone were the days of leaving men behind because they were anchored by their surroundings. Gone were the days of windows rolled down in sultry air, bare foot hard on the pedal, the ribbon of interstate a promise and a heartbreak all in one. It was time to *grow up*.

After all, I came with my own baggage. I was obsessed with marathon running, maybe as much as he was single-mindedly focused on guns. I trotted down the street in horizontal rain to meet my training partners, running twenty miles through bleak winter days when sensible people stayed home. I disappeared in my kayak when things got rough. I still didn't know how to ride a bicycle or how to swim. Worse, I was afraid to try, since it could mean failing.

I wanted to ask the other women I knew how they managed it. How did they merge into marriage so seamlessly, leaving their wild selves behind? It seemed like a taboo subject. We could complain about the way our husbands flung crumbs from breakfast across the counter, left coffee to bake on their cups, but never how we felt as if we had slipped below the surface of the sea without a sound.

Or maybe it was just me, so I was afraid to ask. Maybe the years of travel had left invisible cracks in my skin, the kind that could not be repaired. Maybe I was unable to do this simple thing, just like I was unable to swim more than a few yards.

I paid for a vacation I couldn't afford. We had always been at our best in other countries. Instead we fought over what to buy as we sat in the grocery store parking lot. We fought about what activities we each wanted to do. I brimmed with energy. If we hiked far enough in the humid north, if we swam for miles in the tropical water, maybe everything that seemed wrong would be fixed. Motion had always fixed things before.

My husband groaned under such relentless cheerleading. He wasn't enthused about being there in the first place. I realized I had dragged him along to a place he did not want to go. He would have preferred to stay home.

He complained about the heat. He didn't want to hike. "I think I'm allergic to sunscreen," he said in an attempt to go back to camp. Reluctantly he hiked up a mountain, but I could tell he was miserable. Other tourists stared at us as he threw down our bags in the airport when our flights were delayed.

I had never argued so much before. I grew up in a house that was still and calm, conflict avoided at all costs. Living with my gentle parents, the worst thing you could do was hurt someone's feelings. This meant you swallowed any irritation as deeply as you could. While I knew that this caused worry and pain to gnaw at your stomach like undigested bile, it seemed better than shouting. On the rare occasions as a teenager when I disappointed my parents, when anger spilled out, there were raised voices, tears, and slammed doors. This was so unusual that a raised voice still made me want to run.

My parents had seemed like parts of the same plant, growing toward the same sun. Used to being on my own, I wasn't sure how to ever get there, or even whether I wanted to get there. It was becoming clear to me that I had gone into marriage the same way I had gone out on the ocean: knowing nothing, expecting to power through the way I always had with everything else. I had gone in with only a vague idea of who my husband was, an outline I had proceeded to fill in with the man I had wanted and expected him to be. He must have done the same with me.

I was too embarrassed to spill my secret. Like not knowing how to ride a bike, like being unable to swim, this seemed shameful, something that I thought I should hide forever. I was forty years old, old enough to know better. I would put a brave face on it, back paddle a little, sum it all up, and gather the courage to move forward.

three

I decided to study the bear hunting guides because I thought they could teach me about belonging, about enduring. I approached them with trepidation: most of them were rough around the edges, hard bitten, quick to anger. They railed against the Forest Service and the way we made them stay in their prescribed areas. They tolerated each other, sometimes erupting into epic shouting matches across boat bows. But I loved their confidence and the way they moved through the land. They slipped between the unseen fabric of land and sea in a way I longed to do. Graceful men with battered hearts on their sleeves, they opened up in the wilderness when our paths intersected. They spoke of the way their lives were broken and how only the wilderness could fix them. I understood. That was why I was there too.

The bear hunting guides knew how to do everything. Troubleshoot a balky prop, set an anchor in sandy bottom, make their way through a tangle of devil's club using only dead reckoning. They walked fast and drank hard and had no backup plan for when knees were shot or lungs began to go. They pretty much just lived in the moment.

"This is my wilderness," they said when we paddled up to their boats, taking ownership by virtue of longevity. What was unspoken: *It's not yours.* They spun tales of being charged on a twilit stream while I looked over my shoulder, expecting to see the eyes of bears. In previous lives, they had fought in wars that had been only images on my childhood television screen.

Though I could never shoot a bear, I wanted to see what made the guides tick. I wanted to feel as at home out there as they did. I wanted to study the different shades of evergreen that marched along the beach and know the names of each one. I wanted to know that I would be out here today and the next day, and the day after that.

I watched the bear hunting guides as they strode down the docks, rifles over their shoulders. There were few women among them. Most of their wives or girlfriends were shadowy figures left behind on the beach. The men talked about their guns more than their women. They tucked their chins in tight along the rifle stocks, gulped in a breath, and held it. Their fingers gently touched the trigger, sighting in. They babied their guns in a way I never saw them do with anyone or anything else. It was a rare moment of tenderness, a contradiction.

When I bought a gun because it had become clear I needed more practice on the range, they became coaches and cheerleaders.

"Bolt action?" they wanted to know. "How does it shoot?" They offered to help me sight it in. They gave me tips on how to pass my yearly rifle test: "Take a breath and hold it. No, not like that. Don't flinch!" The recoil, they said, was never as bad as you thought. Somehow, I could listen to them the way I never had been able to with my husband. There was less at stake here. A missed shot was not the end of the world.

Often, they talked about getting out, away from the punishment of boats in the swell, fingers raw from salt water, bad backs, recalcitrant clients. "I'd like a place up the East Fork of the Salmon, down in Idaho," they said, or, failing that, someplace in the Southwest, someplace it never rained.

"One more season," they said. But even as they said it, I knew they did not believe they would ever leave. They loved it out here too much. There was no retirement plan for guides; they barely scraped by, something always broken on the boat, each season a gamble. They would stick with it until they died, they said with a grin, until they fell over in their boots.

Most of them had no governor; they pushed themselves hard regardless of age or weather. When I went along as an observer on one trip, we barely ate. I melted cheddar cheese on hunks of bread and brought it to the guide and his client as they stood in the wheelhouse, scanning the shore with heavy binoculars. They brushed the food aside. They ran on something else.

We left the boat and hiked up a stream's flank, hunkering down in the forest for hours, waiting. The client and I fidgeted as a light snow dusted our boots, but the guide sat poised and still, not moving. Below us salmon sluggishly moved upstream, a last-ditch attempt to make it to their home water to spawn. Even where the current flowed against them or where they foundered on the shallow rocks, they kept at it, flapping their tails in a desperate attempt to regain momentum. They were not beautiful fish, eyes milky, skin falling off their bones. No bears appeared, perhaps sensing our presence.

I didn't agree with trophy hunting, especially not hunting of brown bears. The guides slit open the hide and took it along with the skull, leaving the meat, which nobody ate. The carcass lay in the woods where the animal had fallen, the skinned body looking eerily human. It was all about the biggest bear they could find. Their clients paid $16,000 for a ten-day hunt, and on day nine the pressure was on.

This wasn't hunting to me, not really. Doing this, you glassed the beaches and waited. Sometimes you hiked up the salmon streams, but mostly you stayed close to the ocean, waiting for the bears to come to you. It seemed too easy. Not fair.

"Look on the avalanche slopes," the guides said. They weren't saying that to point out the harsh beauty of the mountain, scoured flat by snow and landslide. Instead, they were pointing out where the early spring bears would be, sticking out with their dark fur coats as they hunted for fresh grass.

They saw the landscape in a different way. To them, it was functional, not beautiful. Bays were assessed according to how easy it was to anchor there, how difficult it would be to launch small boats into estuaries and keep them there, how sheltered they were against a big swell. Mountains were measured only by the time it would take to hike over them. They were unmoved by scenery, perhaps because they had grown so used to it.

The biggest bears seemed to know the hunters were there. They stayed away, avoiding the estuaries. A guide told me they became almost nocturnal, moving through the woods at a time when none of us would be onshore. Most of the ethical guides would not let their clients shoot sows, so an entire hunt could pass without a single shot fired. The clients met their fate with understanding or with rage.

The bear hunting guides barged into the office, camo jackets dripping puddles on the carpet. They came without appointments, demanding attention. Why was I allowing the bird-watching guides to bring clients onshore when their scent would linger for days, keeping bears away? Why did I let the other guide, the one they hated, hunt in the same bay? It was their bay, they insisted. Nobody else should have it. The sight of another boat whipped them into a frenzy. Alaska, they complained, was changing, too many people where once it was only them. The sport fishermen were taking all the crabs and prawns. Not to mention that you used to be able to catch halibut but now they were fished out. There wasn't enough space for everyone.

It quickly became apparent that this part of my job was a thankless one, keeping these wild men in check. One of the guides sighed as he shook my hand. "You're the fifth person that's been in charge of this since I started," he said. It was true: a steady stream of my predecessors had fled with only a couple of seasons under their belts.

I knew what else he was thinking. What did I, a recent transplant, know about their lives? Surely, I would leave soon. With a stroke of a computer key I affected the rest of their days. No matter whether it was Forest Service policy, I was the one they blamed. They shook their heads, clenched their fists, stormed out the double doors. They wrote angry letters full of capital letters and exclamation points.

Still, we sometimes found things we could agree on. Sometimes, we were the only people out there. Entire bays iced over, the freshwater streams letting out slowly onto the sea until plates of ice formed. The boats cut through the ice with a jangle of musical notes. It was impossible not to marvel at things like this, no matter how hardened you had become. And we all needed wilderness, for our own reasons.

The men who piloted the midsize cruise ships were different. Their livelihood depended on showing jaded tourists spectacles every day, and this place delivered. They brought people to the beaches where they could marvel over spruce trees so wide that three men could not touch fingertips around the base. They hiked up to the unnamed waterfalls, several stories high. These guides pestered me for more. They needed miracles, extravaganzas to show their people. They wanted more trails, more places to go where other people weren't. They complained about the bear hunters, boiled into my office when shots were heard.

The locals, on the other hand, were as wary as easily spooked fish. They had perhaps seen too many like me, people who came looking for something and left without finding it. "Most people come here looking for something, or escaping something," one man told me. "But everything you want to escape, you end up bringing it with you." Now I realized he was right. Being here hadn't made me a different person. I was the same woman I had been before, the one I had always disliked for my reluctance to commit to a place or a person, for the things that made me different.

I would begin by making ocean friends, I thought. Like mountain friends, these were the people you called when a benign sun poked out from the other side of Kruzof Island. You paddled together into the Western Channel, around the rocky confines of the airstrip, and way out the causeway. When you paddled with someone, you learned a lot. You saw how they handled a surf landing, a sudden wake. You saw whether they raged over wet feet or took them in stride.

Something about being in the ocean made people open up like flowers. Over a few miles of paddling you could begin to know someone better than you ever could inside four walls.

Friends, I thought, would fill in the gaps. My kayak partners would make up for the loss of the best friend I had thought to gain through marriage. With enough of them, I could stop asking my husband for things he was unable to give. With enough of them, I could still the critical voice in my head. I could blend myself into this place so tightly that the desire to leave would be completely gone.

sweep stroke

It is harder than it looks to turn a boat in a one-eighty. You can sprawl all over the ocean if you want to, but a sweep stroke is the better way.

You have to get a little bit uncomfortable to do a sweep stroke. You need to lean on an edge, enough to help with the turn but not enough to flip. Look up toward your feet and place your paddle into the water at a spot roughly parallel to them. Swing the paddle decisively in a curve toward the stern. This is a stroke you need to put some muscle behind. The more determined you are, the faster your boat will swing around.

When would you need a sweep stroke? Perhaps your kayaking partner is in trouble and you need to go back. Maybe they are trying to point out deer swimming between islands. Or perhaps you have lost your way and you must return to the last place that feels familiar. That's when a sweep stroke comes in handy.

one

I lay sleepless in the tent on the first night of a five-day kayak wilderness patrol, the rifle beside me. The tide was coming in, creeping with delicate fingers over the cobble beach, sweeping the stranded ocean creatures and the driftwood back out to sea. Rain fell in intermittent bursts on the tarp stretched above the tent. Listening closely, I could hear the heartbeat of the ancient forest: the sweep of dense branches as the trees circled overhead in a dance with wind, the mouthfuls of rain gulped down by the dark soil below their roots.

Helga and I had set up our tents close to a bear trail, not by choice but by circumstance, the cliffs a dizzying plunge into ocean, hardly anything flat for miles. We found this small slice of beach, curving up into a spruce forest, and pulled our kayaks far from the tide line, securing them with rope to logs buried in sand. We had forced our tents into the space between beach fringe and water, the bear tracks close enough to nearly reach out and touch.

I curled around cold steel like a lover, my talisman for a safe night. The rifle, a .375 H&H (Holland & Holland), was tough to carry in the field. The sling slipped off my shoulder and it was hard to manhandle through brushy cedar thickets and while balancing on slick rocks in the intertidal zone. It had to be babied, massaged with oil, cotton patches pushed through the guts after I fired it, no matter how long the day had been. I did not have the patience for it.

There was nowhere good to carry it in the kayak. It was too long for the hatches. Keeping it fastened to the deck made the boat unstable. I ended up shoving it down in the cockpit with the bags of trash, where it got in the way and lay in a puddle of salt water.

Moe, who did the end-of-season maintenance, frowned when I showed up. "Why is this rifle so rusty?" he wanted to know. He sent me off with oil and a bunch of rags. "You have to treat the rifle right. It might save your life," he lectured.

I didn't like shooting it at the range either. There was not enough meat in the place below my shoulder where the rifle needed to go, and I ended up with bruises from the recoil. It was loud, too, and I flinched in anticipation, my shots ending up low and to the right.

Because the Forest Service required me to carry it, I complied, although I was not sure I would be able to shoot a bear if things went wrong. Guns were so casual in town, a second thought; people carried them the way women carried purses in other states. A newcomer to guns, before each practice shot, I hesitated: the spiral of the shell out of the barrel seemed so final, something I couldn't take back.

A few years before, one of the timber cruisers had shot a bear that had circled him in the woods before charging. The bear fell seven feet from his boots. Then there were the stories people passed around at night: the hunter attacked near the waterline in Port Alexander, his screams heard by his companions, who promptly ran to the village to drink themselves into a stupor before attempting rescue. Another man found mauled, alone in a remote bay, signs of a struggle; a man knocked off his bicycle. I remembered them all in my tent.

"Hang in there, Gertrude," I said aloud. Gertrude was my alter ego; a burly sidekick I had recently invented to somehow embody the guts and stamina a visitor should possess in this wild place. Gertrude had no soft underbelly. She had no inner critic. She carried a rifle easily and did not lie awake wondering what was making the noise outside the tent. She dove into life headfirst. Sometimes I was her. Other times I wanted to give in, collapse in a heap, escape the endless rain, the shivering in damp layers of clothes, the clammy darkness, and the constant vigilance I needed to maintain out here.

A shuffle in the woods brought me half upright, switching on my headlamp. "What's that?" I called out.

"Just me, getting up to pee," Helga said.

Helga was a tiny spitfire, topped with a spray of golden hair. I had gotten lucky when I had found her as my usual kayaking partner. Athletic and direct, she was able to tie bowlines, carry a loaded boat across an estuary, and say what she meant all at the same time.

Helga was as unspooled as I was wound up tight. While I worried over the consequences of a steep southern swell that tossed our boats around like driftwood, when I fretted about the humpback whales that could easily knock us into an unforgiving sea, she remained as unruffled as the water in a protected bay. If a bear came in the night, she reasoned, that meant our time was up. She didn't lie awake the way I did. She had seen her share of heartbreak, but she shrugged it off better than I could. Things happened; uncharted rocks scraped the bottom of your boat, bears chose the same path you did. Your heart broke sometimes. You just went on.

I knew that there were things in the night that a tent couldn't keep out. If Helga knew that too, she did not say so.

On the outer edge of our bay, the part that faced the sea, waves worried the rocky beach. Beyond us, back in the woods, I sensed that bears moved like the ghosts of the people we had been before we had come to Alaska to shed our skins.

At home, the house was brightened only by the lightning flash of pass-ing car headlights. The air was stale with the smell of someone long gone, someone who cast off dripping boots and clothes, changed, and left again. My husband was out on the ocean somewhere, working the downriggers. He never released the fish he caught. He even caught humpies, the fleshy dog salmon that nobody else wanted. He stacked the bodies in the cooler like insurance against starvation, though our freezer overflowed. He came home only when he had to, when the tide change and the darkness drove him back to shore. When he spoke to me, his words were never of love but only of problems: the need for a new kicker motor, a gun that wouldn't fire, the price of diesel.

At the gun range the next week, I slammed the bolt shut and fired at the targets, Moe wielding a stopwatch to make sure I hit all three in less than twenty seconds. It would never be second nature, the recoil that knocked me half a step backward. After all this time I should have expected it, a sudden blow to the shoulder. After all this time I should have expected a blow to the heart too, every time I came home. But I kept at it, lining up my sights the way I had been taught, trusting that next time it would be different. I would be Gertrude, free, unafraid, needing nothing but a kayak and a following sea. It would work for me the way it did for other people, the bullet straight and true, effortless, the gun light as air.

two

As we paddled through the Myriad Islands, we found gifts from the sea. Long-range ocean currents, swirling around the Gulf of Alaska, had brought us bath toys fallen off container ships, big-lipped yellow ducks and green turtles. White hard hats were sprinkled like snow through driftwood piles, and I imagined a crew of bareheaded construction workers some-where, wondering where their helmets were. We picked the hard hats up and settled them on our salt-encrusted heads, posing in them, until there were so many that they were no longer a novelty. A shipment that had nev-er arrived, I thought, the intended recipients left wondering.

We kicked through the detritus with our rubber boots, calling to each other, detailing our finds.

"More Japanese shampoo bottles over here!"

"Hey! Look, a computer monitor."

If we were lucky, we found blue-tinged, translucent orbs, fishing floats that had escaped from long-ago nets on the other side of the world. Some of these things, I knew, had taken years, decades, to get here to some nameless beach. I imagined them bobbing out there somewhere unknown, pushed by unseen currents day after day, year after year. Why this beach, why this island? Sometimes, sifting through all the things we found, I was overcome by how random it all was.

Part of our job as kayak rangers was to pick up trash, but we knew we could not fit all the beach drift in our boats, so we concentrated on what campers had left behind. We collected tarps that flew like sails as we tried to collapse them into manageable piles. We picked up fire-scarred tin cans, shotgun shells, and lawn chairs. Our boats wavered, unstable with all the weight piled on the decks.

Poking around, we found signs of people who had lived and died here: ancient canoe haul-outs, smooth patches of beach where the Tlingit had painstakingly moved rocks aside to pull up their long canoes, grave-stones tilting drunkenly on little islands, remains of wooden longhouses. We ducked into the beach fringe and stumbled upon rails with ore carts still poised upon them. We peered into adits full of dark, deep water. We uncovered log cabins shorter than I was, slumbering in the woods. I took photographs of what others had left behind; in the winter, I would write up reports for the archaeologist on what remained.

The islands were mostly empty now, but years ago hundreds of people had been here, scattered through the bays and inlets we now paddled. This island, Chichagof, Shee Kaax, had seen the eager and the desperate: gold miners on a large and small scale, cannery workers, fox farmers who lasted until the fur market went under, and families who came hoping for better lives. Their dwellings stood mute and forgotten. Of the Tlingit, who were there first, there were few signs. The big, wet forest had a way of reclaiming everything. The archaeologist, back in town, knew this. He accepted my reports and pictures with a sigh. What I wrote up was ephemeral, a lost history that receded more each day.

≈

We paused in our boats on the edge of the island chain, calculating. Going outside the protection of the Myriads meant exposing ourselves to the brunt of the sea. There were few places to duck back in, just long stretches of dark cliffs and wave-pounded rocks. But there were also hidden slices of beach that nobody ever saw, accessible only to kayaks. The lure of the unknown had always been impossible for me to resist.

"It looks good," I said. The ocean was flat calm, the sky and sea nearly the same color, as if we were trapped in an inverted gray bowl.

"It's hardly ever like this," I said, a promise, a dare. Helga gazed back, her eyes ablaze. With each dip of my blade, I was becoming more about the exploration and less about the consequence. The ocean was teaching me how to let go. I was learning to slip out of my fear.

Our boats left a foamy wake as we pointed our bows south. We had not checked in with dispatch; they wanted us to call in every half hour while we were on the ocean, a policy that put us at risk while we were negotiating the waves. I resolved to call in as much as I could while staying safe. I wanted nothing that could hold us back.

We were bounded only by sea and land and our imaginations. To the west all I could see was the ocean ironed flat. Out on the three bleached rocks the charts called the White Sisters, hundreds of sea lions bellowed in a constant chorus.

"Don't you want to just turn right and keep paddling until you come to something?" I asked. "Japan, maybe?" But Helga hadn't heard. I turned my gaze to the islands to our east.

We had once walked the headlands we now paddled past, hiking a hundred feet above the sea, our feet sinking deep into emerald moss. We found things there too: skeletons of winter-killed deer, blue-tinged feathers from unknown birds. Once we left the beaches, it was easy to believe we were the first humans to ever traverse the higher cliffs.

A dense curtain of rain approached from the south. Helga had forgotten her rain jacket and wore an ancient wool sweater. "I'll just stay under the trees," she had shrugged, but of course she couldn't, not when we were miles from our next camp. It didn't matter anyway. This kind of rain was relentless and unforgiving. It needled its way into whatever gear we wore. We were slick with rain; it rolled down our spines and into our rubber boots. Our tents dripped with our trapped breath. After a while there was no middle ground between dry and wet. We gave ourselves up to the rain.

Helga was pregnant that summer and we stopped often to eat, floating in our boats as we gobbled down bagels gone soft from the wet air, trail mix in damp plastic bags. Trudging up into the forest to pee, we sang pieces of songs we remembered to keep the bears away.

"I won't be able to do this next summer," Helga said, her gesture taking in everything: the islands, the big sea. She didn't seem to mind the way I would have.

I had never wanted children; to me they were like the anchors I threw out on the motorboat, the long, heavy chain spooling out from my outstretched arms, a tug as the boat was irrevocably stopped. How did people stand it? I eyed her as she paddled, sensing that a gap had opened between us. Where she had gone, I could not follow. Instead I would inherit younger women, faces untouched by sorrow, women who would go on to have their own babies and would turn away from the sea. Soon, I imagined, I would be fifty, sixty years old, still out here.

When I thought this, I seesawed between fear and desire. I knew that this kind of life was one I had always dreamed of. There was a thin line between life and death out here, and I had become good at walking it. I even craved it, that sense of being completely alive and present in the moment, a series of questions to answer: how high the swell, how aggressive the current, how many bears onshore. Not for me granite countertops, hand in hand at Ikea, the seemingly mind-numbing routine that all of my former seasonal friends had fallen into without a sound.

But as we paddled, Helga talked about the piece of land she and her husband were buying on another island. For a getaway cabin, she said. I braced my paddle against my cockpit, watching drops fall like pearls, absorbed by the sea. A small sliver of me wanted that too, someone to pore over maps with, to walk the land drawing up plans.

I didn't talk about my own marriage. I didn't say that sometimes I wondered whether something in me was broken; I had been traveling light for so long, I didn't know how to pick up all the messy pieces that came with loving someone. I had left so many men behind as I traveled the country that the reasons for leaving were easier than the ones for staying. The voice in my head was right: I was unable to commit to a person or a place. Instead I was silent, adding more discarded things to carry home. Each time I was in the Myriads I resolved to be a person who carried things with her instead of jettisoning them for someone else to pick up.

My husband was beginning a tactical retreat. He surrounded himself with sound: the television, tuned to a sports event; the computer playing music; a radio in the garage. He erected these barriers against me and my attempts to scale the walls he had built around himself. When I came home, he no longer greeted me at the door. Instead, he stayed put in a fortress of noise. I was blindsided by how, so quickly, things had gone wrong.

But it was hard not to feel hopeful in the Myriads. The islands sprawled out from the larger Chichagof Island, as big as a mainland, as if someone had picked up handfuls of cobble and forest and thrown them in a wide arc. With each stroke of the paddle we uncovered new mysteries: Who had lived on this fox farm and why had they left? Who had walked this beach before us and what had they left behind?

The rain fell harder until it beat the water in a tight staccato, pockmarking it with hundreds of tiny holes. The wind whipped up without warning and a light chop bounced under our boats. Just in time, we ducked into the hidden passage that led to the larger island where we would camp.

When the sun came out, if it ever came out, it turned the tips of waves to rows of sparkling diamonds. We lay back in our boats with our feet propped on the bow, our clothes steaming, our faces upturned, soaking the sun into our bones to save up until the next time. There were entire months when the sun never punched through the clouds. It was better to accept this than fight it. I knew that somewhere it was summer, places where people did not wear wool mittens and hats at night; where you could strip down past the long underwear layer. But not here, and I believed that made us tougher somehow.

Sometimes as we walked the beaches, I scanned what was left behind, adding up what I could use in case we were stranded: ropes and plywood for shelter, discarded life jackets for warmth. I added up the food we could collect here: fiddleheads, sweet beach asparagus.

If we had to, I thought, we could live out here forever.

As we rounded the island, the land curving like a woman's belly, I noticed a fin slice the water. "Whale," I whispered, and we floated as close as we dared. I knew that one shrug of the gray whale's shoulder could sink us, but it was easy to also believe we were invincible. Sometimes it was easy to forget that I was not part of the sea. On land, unloading our gear, I stumbled at first, clumsy and uncertain.

Soon we saw the whale blow a hundred feet away; it had slipped silently up the island without us knowing. I let out my breath like I imagined the whale did, long and slow and quiet. Soon we would paddle to a beach and pull our boats far beyond the reach of the tide. We would reach deep into the hatches and unload all the gear we carried to protect us from the rain and the bears and the cold. We would see no other people, although all around us would be souvenirs brought to us from the sea; belongings lost or forgotten or dumped by people we would never know, entire lives we could never imagine or believe.

three

Helga and I resembled oversize ballerinas, still wearing our spray skirts as we stood on our sea legs, rubber boots sinking into a soft sand beach. Just in from the combination of wind and tide that had turned placid Chatham Strait into towering gray waves that rushed up behind our boats, surfing them forward, we were unsteady and battle worn. We had fought the swells the entire seven miles from our last camp, spray coating our hair as though our heads had been dipped in salt. The slender throat of Gut Bay had swallowed us in along with the flood tide.

Once inside, the bay opened up like a gift, unwrapping itself as we moved deeper inside until we were enclosed inside its heart, a circular expanse of sheer gray cliffs and water the same untroubled color as the sky. The white-topped head of Mount Ada towered over us, less than a mile high but from our level appearing to be many times that.

We were here to do a campsite inventory; record all the subtle signs that others had slept here before us. It was called establishing a baseline, a way of seeing into the future. In five years, maybe more, we could come back and see what had changed. Were there more campsites, indicating more use of these bays? Were people leaving more trash, or were their feet grinding out the vegetation at an increasing rate? With that knowledge, we could make a plan. What that plan would be was unknown: maybe it could lead to more rangers to patrol the coast; maybe we could launch an education program to teach campers how to choose durable sites, stop hacking branches from trees, and avoid campfires that burned deep into the roots and soil. In wilderness, the undefined concept of solitude ruled. As managers, we were supposed to provide it, and while this wild coast held more solitude than anywhere I had ever been, I was aware of how fragile this place was. By inventorying the campsites, we could show their density in one particular bay, thus extrapolating how quiet and remote a visitor's experience could be. It was simple math: the more campsites, the less solitude a person could find.

Helga laughed as I slipped off my rubber boots and hung my bare feet over the sides of the cockpit. We stroked through water shot through with sunlight, the restless ocean floor unseen hundreds of feet below. It seemed impossible that just a few moments before, we had been bracing in high seas, struggling with wind and current. Here there was none of that. Every time Helga dipped her paddle, I could hear the gurgle of water eddying around it. Behind us two narrow V-shaped wakes slowly widened and flattened until all signs of our passage were invisible. I imagined that we were invisible too, so small in the vastness of mountain and sea.

At the very end of the bay an estuary lay naked, disrobed by the low tide. I knew from studying the tables that tides were extreme here, a difference sometimes of twenty feet between the high and low, but it was difficult to understand until I saw it like this.

Our kayaks ground to a halt at the place where the mudflat met the ocean, a level expanse that reeked of fish and secrets laid bare, soon to be covered again. It was filling in now, the tide as slow as a dream. At the far side of the estuary, a wide-mouthed river tumbled into the bay. Beyond all that, an endless forest marched to the west. Past that, uncrossable mountains. If there were campsites, they would be here.

A bear the color of dark chocolate grazed the summer sedges, two cubs shadowing her. They stopped and gazed with unconcern as the tide flowed under our boats, setting us free. Though it looked like good camping far back under the trees, I waffled.

"Bears," I pointed out unnecessarily. Helga shrugged. The specter of a bear in the night didn't haunt her as much as it did me. She humored me, picking up her paddle and beginning a retreat. The campsite inventory of this estuary would have to wait until the bears left.

We found the beach halfway up the bay. A half-moon of white sand ringed by slender-stemmed grass, it would be as gentle on the fragile skin of our boats as it would on our sleeping backs. Typically, we cursed the round beach cobbles that twisted our ankles. Covered with a slimy layer of kelp, the rocks caused us to slide around like ice skaters as we fought to keep our balance with armloads of gear. Driftwood compounded the problem, stumbling blocks between us and any flat spot we could consider a suitable campsite.

This country wasn't made for camping like other places I had known. Here there were no welcoming pine flats or lazy river corridors with plenty of elbow room. Here you had to be resourceful and determined. You didn't pass up a good campsite here, because the next one might be ten miles away.

We floated just offshore in a few inches of water, pondering our options. "Let's camp here," I decided, turning in. Helga was game, and we beached the boats to begin the unloading process. I had learned from my first disastrous trip to pack in numerous small dry sacks instead of larger ones that wouldn't fit the hatches right. You wanted to use every bit of air that you had, with angular bags that conformed to the shape of the boat. The heavier items near the middle, lighter ones to the outside. We carried the stove and food bags to the designated camp kitchen, as far away from our sleeping area as we could get. Slowly the pile of gear dwindled until the beach became our home for the night. Then we knotted a fat rope to a handy log to ensure our boats didn't float off, leaving us stranded.

We sat on the beach eating our couscous and tuna. The rifle lay between us, and I hoped the bears had what they needed at the estuary. Though we had called in by radio to say we were at camp, nobody in the world knew our exact location. There could have been a fishing boat in the next bay, or maybe not for another fifty miles. Whether we lived or died was up to us.

It was the Fourth of July and Helga reached into her pack, bringing out a small flask of whiskey. Cut with the only thing we had, citrus Powerade, it was a vicious concoction, but we sipped it anyway. I thought of our friends in town, doubtless spread across the harbor in their own boats, watching the fireworks bloom over the ocean. Though I sometimes missed the camaraderie that came with a more regular job, we had our own fireworks. On clear nights, meteors exploded across the sky. Humpback whales breached, their entire bodies flipping out of the water in an eruption of spray and sound. Sometimes dolphins arced alongside our boats, paralleling us as we stroked the expanse of Chatham Strait. Even rarer but still possible, the aurora painted the sky in pastel colors. Why would anyone want to be anywhere else but here?

"The tide's still coming in," Helga pointed out. It was true. Without us realizing it, water had crept into the corners of our camp. It had already covered the lower half of the beach and was still on the move. As we watched, unbelieving, it progressed with a slow purpose, indifferent to us, making for the grass where our tents were nestled.

"It'll stop soon," I said, checking the time, but there was still an hour to go before the point when the surrender came, when the tide would draw back again for another six hours. It was clear that our camp was in danger.

Yanking our tents free, we hoisted them over our heads as we shoved them brutally into the spiny brush that marked the end of the beach and the beginning of the cliff. Behind us there was only solid rock. There was nowhere else to go.

I scanned the unforgiving outline of the bay. There were no dimples in the rock walls that could serve as a campsite. If the tide kept coming, we would have to load our boats at high speed, chilly water coming up past our ankles as we hurried. We would have to shove off at twilight and look for another place, most likely sharing space with the bears. I pictured us walking back in the big trees, stumbling over bears as they slept. It was another miscalculation, and I knew that this coast was not lenient with mistakes.

I held my breath. How long should I wait before I called it? Had I already waited too long?

The steady flow of water diminished to a slow amble. Finally, the tide stopped, a foot from our tents. We had been spared, this time.

Helga wandered out to the place where we had first set up the tents. The water almost overtopped her rubber boots. As usual, she seemed unfazed by the recent events. We had moved our tents in time, we hadn't drowned, our sleeping bags were dry—what was the big deal? As usual, I fretted over what could have been. I pondered the horror of waking up to tents afloat, the sea our mattress. I still knew little of tides, unsure of how to translate numbers to landscape. The water moved fastest in the hour before high tide, I had heard, claiming an inch a minute, but I had underestimated just how fast that was. Surely this was something the old hands knew, the difference between flood and ebb and when you were safe. As I watched the water slowly relinquish its hold on the beach, I was sure of only one thing: even now, after a few seasons here, I had so much more to learn.

The next afternoon I listened for the sound of a plane that never came. We paddled to the estuary, the bears now gone, and recorded a few small campsites with rock fire rings. On our tiny beach, we busied ourselves with chores: bundling up the trash, unloading shells out of the rifle. When we were finished, there was nothing to do but lob rocks into the water and wait. Our pickup time came and went with no explanation. It was a clear, sunny day with just the hint of a breeze, perfect flying weather.

I knew that conditions could be completely different on the other side of the island. This one received the brunt of the snow, the heavy-bellied clouds dumping their loads before rising to take on the mountains. It also got slammed with rain. Little Port Walter just down the coast bore the dubious honor of being the wettest place on Baranof Island, with over 237 inches of mixed rain and snow per year. Out of all the days of the year, almost three hundred brought some form of precipitation.

Finally, my handheld radio crackled to life. "The plane can't make it to Gut Bay," the dispatcher said. "Fog up the coast. Maybe tomorrow. Get to a place where they can see you and throw out something colorful."

We looked at each other in dismay. We had to make a move and do it soon. Our tide-ravaged beach would not work for a pickup, and we had been flirting with high water anyway. The tide was predicted to rise much higher than it had the night before. At any rate, our camp was too far back in the bay and hard to pick out from the air. The word from dispatch was firm: get to the head of the bay where we could be seen. They couldn't give us a pickup time, so we would have to be prepared. In this big country, it was easy to be missed. I had seen this when we did our complicated kayak shuttles. Diving down into the bay in a floatplane, I had squinted, trying to pick Helga out where she waited with our gear, but the forest stretched out, unbroken. Only when we got within feet of landing could I see her.

With fully loaded boats, we paddled to the front of the bay. Here there was no softness in the rock walls that catapulted to the sky. Mount Ada rose steep sided and impervious, casting a late afternoon shadow across the water. It would be night soon and I didn't relish the idea of scouting with headlamps. It would be too easy to break bones on the steep terrain or surprise a wandering bear. Because we were on the inside, there would be no kelp beds to raft up in, a practice I had heard about from some long-distance paddlers who had needed to catch a few moments of sleep. According to them, if you wedged your boat in just right, you were ensnared firmly, safe for a time.

There was no going out of the bay either. The storm outside had calmed, but the next bay was too far down the coast to make it to tonight. We hugged the shore, looking for possibilities.

I remembered my first trip with Mark and Rowan, my heart sinking as each island slid by. Then I had been too picky with my campsites, expecting the same flat landscape I had become accustomed to down south. By now I was a master of small spaces. We had shoehorned our tents into tiny overhangs, sandwiched between beach and forest, sometimes on such a slant that we slid across slippery tent floors all night long.

"Maybe right there?" Helga suggested. I looked where she was pointing with her paddle. A slight indentation in the cliff led upward to a pair of table-sized rocks, wedged firmly, I hoped, into the surrounding cliff. It looked like a go, and it was all we had.

We pulled our kayaks onto the rocks and scouted. "If one of us puts a tent here, on this rock, and the other can fit near the roots of this spruce, I think we can do it," I said. Laboriously we handed gear up the cliff's gullet, dodging rocks and hauling our boats over our heads to wedge them in between a pair of boulders. I shoved my tent into a tree that somehow grew out of this stony outcrop, bending the poles as much as I dared. Helga balanced her tent on a flat boulder, tying off her guy lines to tree branches.

We looked at our makeshift camp and laughed. We were a pair of wilderness hoboes.

"We might have to pick you up and take you to Juneau and get you a commercial flight home," dispatch said as we relayed our position. It appeared that conditions were still unsettled on the other side of the island.

"What about the rifle? We can't get on the plane with a rifle and no case," I said as we sat on our respective rocks. "And all of our gear. It's not in big bags. How could we put it on a commercial flight?" I could feel myself winding up to a meltdown. I hated when I did this, but sometimes the worry that simmered inside me rose to a boil. At those times obstacles seemed insurmountable.

Helga sighed. "Why are you always worrying about things that might not happen?"

"I'm just planning ahead," I snapped. She raised an eyebrow; this was the closest to a fight we would ever get. Like worrying, arguing was a waste of Helga's time. She preferred to deal with the here and now. It was an attitude I would do better to emulate, I knew.

I lifted a mug of hot chocolate to my lips. How did you change, if you wanted to? My husband insisted he could not change, but I knew there had to be a way to break free of the patterns you had sewn yourself into. You had to want it badly enough to stop your forward momentum and turn around.

In a frosty silence, we tended to our respective camps, but Helga never held a grudge for long, and because she couldn't, I couldn't either. We had been buddies for a while now, long enough to weather a small storm. Under soft pink sunset, we climbed back down to our boats and went for water, pausing under the narrow throat of a waterfall and holding out our bottles.

The next day I talked the plane in, narrowing down a massive chunk of ground to our tiny dot on a map. We threw out the silver sides of our emergency blankets and waved blue tarps over our heads like frantic dancers. "Come down the gut and then fly south; we're in the middle of the west side of the bay in the first large finger," I reported. "At your ten, right now."

The pilot searched fruitlessly until I thought he might give up and go away. At the last minute, we were spotted. As I ferried gear down to the plane, I knew I needed to stop worrying about every last thing. The wilderness was trying to tell me something. Slow down, it said. Breathe. I knew I had to listen. If I listened hard enough, it would tell me how to change.

quartering

A quartering stroke is exactly what it sounds like. Instead of plowing straight ahead in rough weather, you move at an angle to the wind or waves, whichever is your nemesis at the time. This keeps your momentum and helps prevent your boat from being pushed underwater by serious chop. You don't want this to happen, as a bow under the surface means a boat that could cartwheel forward.

You probably won't get to practice this stroke very much because it takes the right combination of wind and wave to need it. Let's hope you have paid attention when you do. Let's hope you don't let your guard down, not for one single second.

one

When the winds approached twenty knots, it was nearly impossible to keep forward motion. It was more effort than it was worth, and it was time to call it quits. We quartered desperately across a fetch, bound for safety.

I had known that the forecast was right on the edge, but I had decided to chance it. There was always the hope that the winds would not be quite as strong as predicted. Helga was a strong paddler and was willing to take it on as well. Since neither of us was a quitter, we found ourselves suspended in open water, fighting to slant our boats into the wind.

"There's an island!" I hollered, seeing a small outcrop up ahead. Helga glanced over but could not decipher my words. I hoped she would follow as I pivoted, trying to maintain my quarter but still gain on the island, which would easily slip past our bows if we did not take action soon.

Quartering was a stroke that Wyatt had not been able to teach us, since you used it only in lumpy seas. He could only try to explain it as we rafted up in the deceptive calm of Silver Bay. Picture this, he told us: the waves stirred up to a light boil, the wind working against them. It was similar to a ferry, but different, since your goal was to prevent the bow from diving deep into the wave, a situation that could tip you or at the very least, toss the boat broadside.

It wasn't a stroke I knew well, but it was instinctual. Once the front of the kayak started to disappear in the chop, I knew to maneuver the bow to angle into the wave instead of taking it head on.

Sometimes when I paddled eight, ten hours a day, I could let my mind slip into the marathon zone, the same place I got to when I ran twenty-six miles. This was a place where the mind and body forgot pain. I didn't feel the grating of rubber gloves on wet skin, the dull ache in my back. I didn't mark each mile by the laborious pull past a craggy headland. Instead, it was as if I had broken through to a layer of light and air where there was no brain, only muscle and heart and bone. As if propelled by some ancient sea-going memory, my body took over completely, unfettered by the constant thoughts and limitations that held it back. At those times my boat flew over the water like an arrow shot from a bow, and when something startled me out of it, a partner calling to me or a troller passing by, I noticed I had gone miles without noting the distance.

I craved this zone like a junkie needing a fix. I had chased it all my life, whether by hiking up mountains all day long, running for hours, or now, paddling. The problem was, I never knew when it would happen, that inaudible click when it all aligned and I slid between awareness and meditation. This desire, I realized now as I lined the boat up for another run at the chop, was what had kept me traveling for years past most other seasonal workers' expiration dates. In a regular job in a regular life, how often could you get there?

It was not happening today, not with quartering. You could not let your mind wander for a single second. I was limp with fatigue as I pulled my boat onto the welcome gritty sand of the tiny island. I knew that if we were pinned down here it would be a long wait, since we could stride across it in less than five paces. But it was protected and would serve as a refuge for now. We could regroup here and come up with a strategy.

Sandy beaches were often the best places to camp, but they also often sloped gently down toward the water, which made for an uncomfortable night of sliding downhill in a tent. Luckily, I had recently learned a technique for avoiding this.

"We've found the Southeast Alaska campsite trifecta," I raved as we carried gear up the beach. "Sunshine, a sandy beach, no bears."

As expected, our camp spot, just outside a ragged line of trees, was not level. Taking a flat piece of driftwood, I set about preparing something better. Raking the wood deep into the sand, I scooped out a flat place for the tents.

"Voilà, camp!" I announced, shaking out my wet tent. This small disturbance would last only as long as the next big winter tide.

Satisfied, we sat down on a log and surveyed our surroundings. From the safety of our island we could see the line of whitecaps stretching past Herbert Graves Island and into the next channel. Foam spit off the tops of the waves, a sure sign of increasing wind. Overhead, high cirrus clouds flung themselves across a pale sky. All things pointed to a windy evening.

But that was fine. We were safe, and we had filled our containers with freshwater as we passed an old fox farm site hours earlier. There was nowhere we had to be. I dug my bare toes deeper into the sand and sighed with contentment. Bare toes, a luxury here. Except, what cold and slimy thing had they just touched?

I glanced down at the sand next to me and screamed. Sitting there as if someone had placed it was a volleyball, painted to look exactly like Wilson in the movie *Castaway*. I picked it up and examined it.

"Creepy," Helga said, and I had to agree. Our island no longer seemed quite as serene. Had someone else been stranded here when a volleyball floated in from the tide? Had someone chucked it overboard from a passing ship? It was another one of those wilderness mysteries that we would never be able to solve. These riddles could occupy us for hours as we paddled past some unchanging, monotonous shore.

We strolled to the other side of the island. The trees here were thin and battle worn from constant struggle against the salt spray that catapulted from the arms of the wind. This side was not landable, fronting an open passage, waves dashing themselves against the rocks.

"A flushing bay," I observed. Helga knew what I was thinking. A flushing bay was where you dropped your drawers to poop, the thought being that the ocean could handle a little waste better than the land. It required luck and skill to do this without getting soaked, and it always felt a little weird. You had to scan the horizon to ensure that a small cruise ship wasn't passing by or that a fishing boat wasn't anchored quietly in an unnoticed corner. Old-timers, I knew, still went well offshore in boats and dumped plastic bags of garbage instead of carrying them back to town. I wondered how long we could continue to drop what we no longer wanted in the sea.

After a magnitude 9 earthquake struck Japan in 2011, a ghost ship had appeared off the Sitka coast. The *Ryou-Un Maru* floated free for over a year in the restless Pacific, a boat over 150 feet long, without lights to warn other mariners. With its nine-thousand-liter cargo of fuel, it was an uncontrolled disaster waiting to happen.

A Coast Guard cutter approached and fired at the disabled ship with an autocannon, sinking it and the fuel onboard in six thousand feet of water. It remained somewhere out there on the ocean floor.

I wondered how many other ghost ships remained that we could not see, slowly drifting rudderless through the Pacific.

Night fell as deep and thick as velvet as we retreated to our tents. By now, after several summers of this, each night felt as familiar as sleeping in my own bed. Better, because on land I had taken to keeping my body on one thin edge, one foot hanging out of the covers as if for a speedy escape. Here, noises still woke me, but I quickly fell back asleep. I no longer scrambled for the rifle when bears strode the beach. Without even realizing it, I had become part of this place in my own small way.

≈

I pulled out my chart and studied it, making a plan for the next day. We hadn't attained our goal because of the weather, so we would have to make up time. Or not. It really didn't matter. We would call in our new coordinates and divert the boat or the plane pickup there. It was no longer important to keep to a strict schedule. The ocean, not us, made up the rules.

≈

The challenge of map reading was to interpret what was on the paper and apply it to the tangible reality of mudflat or line of rocks that broke at high tide. At first, before I learned to read charts, none of it made sense. I couldn't make the ocean fit what I saw on the page. It was a mystery that took time to unfold.

So was my body, a map someone could read to add up the woman I was becoming.

When I looked closely at my right palm, I could make out the faint U shape of a sizzling pump's muffler. Our gung-ho fire crew had been trying to keep a running blaze contained and away from multimillion-dollar homes on Florida's Sanibel Island. Nervous homeowners skittered up and down the street, getting in our way.

"Are you sure you have this controlled?" they shouted. Jed, our boss, pointed at a torching cabbage palm on the green side of the line and yelled for water. Climbing up on the engine tailgate to grab the hose, I thoughtlessly balanced on the hot muffler. That night I slept with my hand in a bucket of ice, gritting my teeth. But we stopped the fire.

There were more. A set of white parallel lines marched across my leg, just below the right knee. I remembered hanging from my fingernails on a talus slope somewhere in the White Cloud Mountains of central Idaho, scrabbling for purchase among rocks the size and consistency of Grape-Nuts. The whole mountain was unstable and I was falling with it.

Far above me, Harry, my fellow wilderness ranger, having made the wiser choice, bounded along a game trail leading to the saddle. Too late I recalled his advice: take the deer trails. The deer always pick the best way. Panting, I inched upward, not looking down. I swam through the gravel, body planted full length. Falling over the cliff below was not an option. When I finally crawled on top, bleeding and out of breath, he gestured to the lake sprawled below us. No wilderness ranger had ever been there. This was our holy grail, a place so remote that there were no fire rings or litter, not even a footprint. As we sat on the ridge plotting our descent, legs dangling into open air, three bighorn sheep came out of the trees and into the light.

The other knee boasted a circular sunburst, gained from a wild fall over a downed tree as I puzzled over map and compass, not entirely sure where I was. Lightning crashed inexplicably as snow fell in a freak June storm.

Carrying only a day pack, I needed to make my way to the trail crew camp before dark. Somehow in the thick forest I had blundered into the wrong drainage.

Even my teeth hadn't escaped. My right front tooth was an expensive and carefully crafted reproduction of the one that turned gray after a blow to the face from an errant branch while I searched for a safe creek crossing.

Small white patches sprinkled my arms, standing out white around the tan. There was the jagged souvenir of a bout with barbed wire as I crept away from a range bull, my arms full of camping gear. Other landmarks were remnants of scrapes from belly crawls through dank caves, face-plants into lechuguilla cactus, and stumbles into poison ivy.

I had no scars from the ocean—not yet. I knew they would come in time.

I gave up on my hair when I was out on the water. It was typically flattened to my head like a seal's, and I shoved it under a hat most of the time. Since I always forgot a comb, I usually substituted a fork.

I had never had a pedicure. When I last donated blood, the nurse repeatedly stabbed my arm for several minutes. "Don't you use lotion?" she exclaimed. "Your skin is like leather!"

Before I moved to Alaska, I had ventured into a smoky bar called the Rod and Gun Club. A scrawny character sized me up. He had my number right off—the abrupt tan line ending where my socks usually started, bruised shins, and freckles advancing across my sunburned nose. "You must work for the Forest Service!" he declared, waving a Coors. "When's the last time you wore makeup?"

Even with all the scars I carried, out here in the wilderness I was beginning to feel beautiful again. At home, on the beach, I always felt like something was wrong with me. There were so many things I could not do right. I could not bring a smile back to my husband's face. I could not stem the dark moods that punched him down for days. I was beginning to realize that I could not save him, and I might have to save myself instead.

The next morning dawned eggshell blue, the sea a recalcitrant calm. We left Wilson on the beach for some other stranded traveler to find.

Though it seemed calm today, I knew that the ocean was never motionless. The restless relationship between wind, earth, moon, and sun created the chop that had tossed us around the day before and the smooth roll that lifted our boats harmlessly now. The earth and moon could not resist each other, and their magnetic force formed the high tide that nearly swept our tents away.

A few years earlier, a tsunami had roared onto a beach in Thailand, killing hundreds. Even with the warning siren in town, even with the blue and white signs that marked an uncertain evacuation route, I was always aware of the impatient chain of volcanoes that belted the Pacific. There had not been a tsunami in recent memory on my island, but the possibility was always there. It felt like I had to constantly scan the ocean, looking for the right path, the right stroke.

"You could just get a divorce," an old friend said across the miles when I gathered up the courage to call. But like a ghost ship, divorce seemed like a distant point, one you might be paddling toward but never really expected to reach. I always turned back before I got too far. Others could go there, venture out into Peril Strait or way out past the islands. Others could throw off their husbands like old coats they never wanted. My parents had been married forever, and their parents before them. I had given up on so many things; I couldn't give up on this too. I would continue to quarter, I thought, find that sweet spot between the chop and the wind where I could slide all the way through.

two

If my husband were his own star, it would not be the sun. There were days when I froze in the deep chill of our house, looking for radiated affection and light. Instead, he would be one of the icy planets on the edge of the solar system, self-contained and mysterious.

"I'm just wired this way," he lectured, explaining why his heart was off-limits. He wrapped himself in a protective layer so impenetrable that I could not pierce it. His emotions were closely guarded, his thoughts his own.

I was too emotional, he went on, but he thought he might be able to live with it. Maybe, he qualified. He liked solid ground, facts, figures. The shifting tides of fear, sadness, and intimacy were things to be avoided at all costs.

The death of my cat was an example. "You were hysterical," he pointed out, his voice tinged with disapproval. It was true: I had rolled on the floor sobbing so hard I had to fight for breath. This cat had been with me through two moves, in my single days the only living creature that seemed to care whether I came home safely from fighting a fire. The free fall into unrestrained sadness was foreign to my husband. It was only years later that I realized he may have been terrified, knowing that this loss of control lurked within everyone, hoping desperately to contain his own.

Could I live for another forty years with someone and muffle who I really was? I wasn't sure. There were times when I thought the ocean was enough. If I could get out in a small boat for a few hours, I would not notice what else was missing. If I could paddle far enough, past the Eastern Channel and around the curved flanks of the outer islands, maybe all the way to Kruzof Island, that would sustain me.

I realized that I had done a bait and switch without intending it. I had met him when I had been new to Alaska, unsure of my place in such a foreign landscape. I had been willing to accept him the way he appeared to be. To linger in the surface layers. Now, more and more, Gertrude was coming out, a strong-willed paddler who wasn't shy about speaking her mind. No wonder he retreated. This wasn't what he had signed up for.

Besides, I had it easy. There were women in town who escaped to the shelter, somewhere hidden in the maze of streets, address unknown. There were women betrayed, women who vanished, women who took the first ferry off the island. I wasn't that bad off. Surely, I could live with this. Women lived with worse, every day.

I threw myself into my work. My little kayak program was gaining attention. An environmental group that had battled the forest for years saw what I was doing and promised to help, sending citizen scientists to the lakes and bays. An ecologist and I roamed the headlands, discussing how to preserve the natural solitude that existed there in the face of certain change.

As we sat on a cliff discussing the importance of solitude, a cruise ship hove into sight. A hundred people crowded the bow, binoculars trained on our camp. The loudspeaker boomed over the formerly quiet bay, an amplified voice lecturing the tourists on what they were seeing. It didn't matter whether the story was true; they would believe it. That was the thing with stories. They always held the ring of truth. The bear hunting guides said one thing; the locals might say another. It was choosing the right story that was the hard part.

As we sat on the cliff, breath from the cold moss seeping in through my rain pants, it came to me that I had chosen someone who matched my inner voice. The things my husband believed about me were the stories I had always believed about myself. I had chosen him partly because it seemed that I would not have to reveal the part of me I thought was different, the part I had been afraid to show anyone. He didn't want to know me very deeply, so I never had to show him anything but my outer self. Now that I had changed my mind and wanted him to really know me, he did not like what he saw. It was true, too, that I had left so many men behind so I wouldn't have to be known. I had thought that if they saw the real me, they would be the ones to leave. I had always left first.

"Humpbacks," my companion said. He pointed. Far out past the kelp and the place where the sea touched the cliffs, the water erupted with the great dark bodies of whales. They leaped out of the ocean, flipping back in as if a door were gently shutting behind them.

"Probably they're doing that to get rid of sea mites," my companion said, but I chose to think of it another way. I imagined that the whales were jumping for the sheer joy of it. They were celebrating the meeting of air and sea.

These whales have one of the longest migrations of any mammal, stretching for thousands of miles. In the fall as the skies darkened, they left these waters to travel to the more welcoming seas near Hawaii. Some internal clock, much like mine, told them when it was time to go. Another one told them when they were home.

We began to pack up our gear in preparation for descent back to the ocean. Much like the quarter stroke on the water, the walking here had to bend to the land. We angled around the tough little trees that sent out spiky branches to pull at our raincoats, and climbed down the craggy cliffs where there were breaks, even if that meant going the long way. In the beginning, I had trusted the land enough to throw my backpack wildly below me and downclimb. Helga had watched me from above, shaking her head. "We can't climb down there," she said, picking the safer way as I angled down carefully to retrieve my battered pack.

Now I knew the truth. If you barreled along without paying attention, you could end up lost and injured, much like the occasional would-be explorer plucked off these mountains by helicopter each year.

The cruise ship lumbered out of the bay, the tourists already gone from the bows. They had seen all of this scenery on the way in, no need to keep looking. They must have thought they were seeing everything, when there was so much more to discover.

three

The stories of the islands I paddled through were beginning to mean more to me than the maps. The maps were one dimensional, a snapshot. They were hard to read while I was balancing in my boat, calculating the angle of the next wave. The locals knew the land by the stories; that was how they navigated. They also knew what I was learning: that there were long, invisible connections from past to present. It was clear that just settling into a community wasn't enough. You had to be humble enough to know the history. You had to forge connections that would tie you to the flow and ebb of the present.

The boats we paddled had evolved out of a long history of people's bond with the sea. The first Alaskan kayak, called an *iqyak*, was fashioned from driftwood and sea lion skin by Aleutian hunters. The Inuit, in a treeless land, used whalebones and an ingenious system of measurement, shaping each boat to custom fit by the size of a paddler's hips and a little extra. These boats were needle-narrow and fast, not the wide-hipped ones we piloted today. In 1840, when comparing "modern" boats to their forerunners, Bishop Ivan Veniaminov wrote that birds could not outrun the early Aleutian kayaks. A seven-year-old child could easily carry one, he added.

While they were more stable and much heavier, weighing in empty at fifty pounds, our fiberglass boats still followed the ancient design. Those original builders had studied the sea and noted what shape would best ride the swells while keeping a straight tack. Five thousand years later, our boats still had a similar shape to the first ones that plied northern waters.

≈

In 1794, Captain George Vancouver's expedition sailed this side of Baranof Island, leaving place names on many of the bays we paddled. When Helga and I climbed the cliffs overlooking Red Bluff Bay, we found ancient, mossy cairns that I imagined belonged to that time. The cairns tilted as high as our waists. It was easy to believe that a lonely crewman had climbed the cliffs and looked out on the same wide expanse of Chatham Strait as we did now, stacking rocks for navigation or for art.

Floating near an overhanging rock wall in one bay, closer than a motor-boat could get, I spotted the faint red outline of a pictograph, three people in a canoe. In this tree-rich land, the Tlingit had traveled in dugouts, entire trees burned out and carved to float, not kayaks. I pictured the quiet water where I paddled sliced by their canoes, people intent on survival, not the luxury of exploration.

I walked past the remains of their villages, set on headlands at the points where the wind would blow away the notorious white sox, a nearly invisible biting assailant. They had been driven out centuries before, and the campsites I chose were part of a shameful legacy of blood and despair.

Still, I liked to think of us as part of a long chain of explorers, a flexible sinew of tide and wind binding us together. Surely, they had their own stories that I would never know, ways to name and know the coast.

When I had to drive the motorboat, islands loomed out of the fog. Sven gripped the passenger side rail as I barely cleared one clump of rocks. "Just go back the way we came!" he said. It was easy for him to say. He had a map in his head; years of travel along the same routes had worn a groove into his brain. I was lost, spinning the wheel in circles.

The others, old-timers, sighed in annoyance. It was so simple. That island there was this one on the map. See the place where it looked like a shark had taken a bite out of the land? You headed past it and through the notch hidden between the next two islands. Keep to the left, for the love of God! See, it was simple.

There were some stories I never learned. I just saw their aftermath: a kayak cleaved cleanly in half washed ashore at the outlet of Lake Ekaterina; the ribs of a boat sunken deep in sand on another beach. I found the things people left behind: buildings hidden like secrets among the alder at the old Chichagof mine, the tailings slowly sending toxic mercury into the sea. There were old cabins still with clothes on hangers and bulging cans of unknown food on the shelves.

As we moved up and down the coast, I thought about what I had left behind. It did not add up to much. I had skimmed the surface of every place I had lived, leaving barely a trace. If someone had tried to piece together my history, there would be no clues.

I slowly learned the country by the stories, not by the map, although the map was the piece that put it all together. Sometimes I would round a point and remember: this is where one of the ranger boat workers had to abandon her boots, stuck fast in the tidal estuary. This was the place where we collected fiddleheads for dinner.

"See that marker?" Ron asked over the intercom as we flew down the coast, indicating a barrel poised on top of a cliff. "Once one of the other pilots flew up that bay in the fog, thinking it was a different one, one that went through to the other side. Barely pulled up in time before he hit the mountain. Later someone put that marker up so everyone would know."

Sven kept up a steady patter of conversation in the ranger boat, pointing out all the places where people had lost their boats, their cargo, or their lives. This was where a girl had swum ashore after a capsize, he said, indicating the rounded back of an island similar to all the others. Her boyfriend, who had been with her, hadn't made it. There was where two people washed up when their boat sank, the woman living for a week on the island before she was found, going crazy, he said, her mind lost to the wilderness.

"Where is she now?" I asked, horrified.

Sven shrugged. "Institution, I guess."

I stared at the island, indistinguishable moments before, but its rounded shape forever recognizable now.

Others taught me names that were not on maps: Radar Island, Nudie Beach. They pointed out places that had seen tragedy, forever burned into the brain: the outpost where an outlaw, a real one, had lived, giving himself the name Blue Sky and molesting young girls until the law caught up with him. That place where the helicopter crashed years ago, one man forever lost.

These stories were my touchstones and waypoints. Sometimes it felt as though the entire coast were a chain of tales, a book waiting to be read.

≈

Our stories out here were few, at least in terms of permanence. Nothing we did left much of a mark, nothing lasting past the season. Our tent sites, the flattened grasses slowly rising, once a pair of sunglasses left hanging on a branch, a bandanna forgotten at tide's edge. If we built a beach fire, we did it below the high tide, where the water would take it overnight. Anyone trying to track us would see only the disappearing V of water as we paddled away.

I had to be careful in town, though; with only a few thousand souls it seemed everyone watched what you did and made up their own truths about it. It seemed better to slide through unnoticed, but of course you never could. People saw me running for hours on the Harbor Point Road; they passed me climbing the alpine trails and saw me dragging my kayak down to the water. They noticed who was with me, and who was not.

"How come you guys don't run together?" Helga asked, spotting both me and my husband on separate jogs through the forest. I shrugged. It was too complicated to explain.

By now I spent most of my time with my running friends, training for a marathon. Running twenty-six miles had always seemed like an unattainable goal, but my friends were equally as determined as I was. When we paused to gulp down Gatorade as we rounded the stretch by the airport, an hour and a half into our run, I saw in their faces the same fierce dedication I had to the goal. During those twenty-mile runs, the rain whipping at our faces, I could be the person I had bottled up at home. We sang off-key, leapt over guardrails, told each other our secrets. After the run, if the weather looked favorable, I would paddle north while Rowan paddled south. We met under the bridge and figured out a plan for the afternoon.

On this day we paddled in companionable silence through the Eastern Channel. "Should we go in No Thorofare?" she asked. I nodded. A year ago, I would never have attempted this route. One of the old stories was about two kayakers in winter, falling out of their boats and delivered to the dock as frozen blocks of ice. Even in summer, there was reason for concern. If you hit the outlet at high tide, you would be sucked out at high velocity through a series of tight passages. Even a brace could not help you.

We floated for a second in the middle of the Eastern Channel, reading the weather. There had been times when we had crossed the channel in a leisurely manner, the water still as breath, and on the way back had been confronted by steep chop. Those were mildly exciting slogs that took twice as long coming as going. Today it looked fine for crossing, the evergreens onshore dead still.

Rowan looked at something over my shoulder. Her eyes got large and she gestured wildly. I swiveled to see.

An enormous shape loomed out of the ocean behind us. A cruise ship. Certain disaster. All summer, these floating palaces dropped anchor outside town, ferrying tourists to shore on small lighter boats. On those days we were sandwiched between ship and shore, having to dodge in between as camera flashes went off. As it departed, each large vessel was supposed to blast its horn to warn the unwary, and somehow I had missed it.

Though these behemoths looked slow moving, I knew one could be upon us in minutes. Even if they saw us now, by the time the captain made the wheel correction we would be crushed under tons of steel, only a small road bump as the ship churned to the next port. It was doubtful they could see us at all, as low as we rode in the water.

We dug in, paddling with all we had, and cleared the channel with minutes to spare. Unaware of our heroic sprint, tourists crowded the bow, snapping photographs of us as we sat catching our breath, safely out of crushing range. Up in the wheelhouse, the captain gave us a cheerful wave. "Cheated death again," I said as we gathered our paddles and our wits.

We threaded the needle into No Thorofare, riding an incoming tide. It was still the boundary between high and low; we had timed it perfectly. All we had was a little boost to push us into the small bay. As long as we did not linger, this bay was ours.

Suspended in the gentle swell of Sitka Sound, I listened to Rowan tell me stories of her life. She glossed over most of it, enough for me to know that there were some scars.

She stowed her paddle to take a drink of water.

"My first fifty years, it was about pleasing other people," she said. "The next fifty are going to be about me."

I envied her. How did you get to that point? I wanted waypoints, a map. "I'm never going to survive the failure of a second marriage," my husband said, locking me in forever. I thought of Moon Reservoir. How could I be responsible for this? After all, there were still times when it worked. We grilled salmon so fresh from the sea that it tasted like hope. I lit candles against the endless Alaska darkness and listened to the rain beat against the windows as if it were desperate to come in. We were in our own bubble of warmth and light. I looked across the table at my husband and the same warmth seemed to radiate from his eyes. We're going to make it, I thought then. There were nights like that.

I remembered overhearing two women having lunch in some forgotten place years ago.

"Are you in love married or just married?" one had asked the other. I didn't hear the reply, but I had thought at the time that I would never settle for just married. Not me, not ever. How could people get themselves into that predicament?

Now I wondered, was anyone really happy? Maybe everyone was just covering up, pushing through the only way they could. I studied the couples I knew, noticing the casual touch of a shoulder or the subtle roll of an eye. On the trail, running alone one day, I heard voices. Two married friends approached, deep in conversation. We exchanged greetings and I ran on in wonder. *They still talk to each other*, I thought. Why did I think this was so unusual?

There were stories of people who had split up and gotten back together, and stories of people who hadn't. "This place is hard on marriages," Tom had confided before making his own escape. Generally, one person longed to stay and the other longed to leave, and this rift widened with each endless November.

Then there were stories of people who died in strange ways: helicopter crashes into the sea, killed by a bear, lying on the floor alone at night in a Forest Service bunkhouse.

There were people who lived in the forest just above town. Unwilling or unable to live inside four walls, they set up elaborate tarp cities and siphoned water out of the creeks. I saw them sometimes, scurrying along the boardwalk, seeming to be some sort of woodland creature unrelated to the rest of us. There were all sorts of ways a life could go. Some people had it easy, it seemed, a straight-up forward stroke through life. Others had to quarter for every inch they got.

scull

Sculling is a movement that you can easily overdo. It is subtle yet powerful.
Like frosting a cake, you hold the paddle upright and use it as a draw, a way
to draw parallel to someone or something. In a sculling draw, you move the
blade in opposite directions, dancing over the surface of the water. It is a figure
eight instead of just a back and forth, moving the face of the paddle toward the
direction you are sweeping.

The scull needs finesse and patience more than any other stroke. It is easy to
catch the blade wrong and find yourself in a world of hurt. So why do it? Because
once you have accomplished the scull, you will feel like you can do anything.

one

"You're a hard nut to crack," Helga said. We stood in the ankle-deep water
of a muskeg, puzzling over aerial photos. These were the maps we used to
navigate, snapshots in time from a plane passing overhead twenty years
ago. The black-and-white images sometimes corresponded with the landscape, but we knew that things changed. We had seen it ourselves, trees
taking over open spaces, entire hillsides tumbling into the ocean as if someone had taken a knife to them, slicing a piece of cake. But the photos were
the best we had and we squinted at the fuzzy images, hoping for clarity.

Today we were headed to a lake perched two miles above the cobble
beach. There was no trail and no sign anyone had been this way, no real
reason for us to crawl through the alders and climb up the cliffs, except
to see whether we could. That was the perk of being the first wilderness

kayak rangers on this coast. If we could get there, others could. They could chainsaw and hack and climb to the lake, creating a web of trails or maybe an illegal cabin, and we had to document what the place looked like before that happened.

With the numbers of tourists increasing every year, it was likely that the tour companies would start looking for other places to go, those that had not been discovered. This was one of those places. In this spongy soil, just a few hikers in one year would beat in a path, trampling sensitive plants and sending dirt cascading into the streams, choking out the fish and other aquatic creatures. Tough weeds could hitchhike in on their boots, establishing a foothold and outcompeting native plants. It wasn't that I thought nobody should be able to see the lakes we hiked to, but how many was too many? It was a thorny problem I wrestled with every day.

By putting in a GPS track and noting the potential trail route to this pristine lake, I could get ahead of a problem. If a trail started to develop, I could make some choices. Either I would build a real trail, heading off poor routes others would create by installing boardwalks and switchbacks, or I would figure out how to erase the undesirable paths. Either way, I wanted to document what the place looked like now, a hedge against an uncertain future.

At least, that was what I told myself. My coworkers, stuck at the office through lack of either imagination or desire, looked at me knowingly as I hurried past, dry suit in my arms. "Going on another junket?" they asked. They looked trapped, wedged in their cubicles.

"It's not a junket!" I defended myself. "We look for weeds, we clean up campsites, we check guide permits . . ." But even as I stood with tie-down straps, cinching the boats tight for the short ride to the boat dock, I half expected someone to run out and stop me. There was an element of getting away with something every time I launched my boat.

But still, we knew the coast better than most people did. There was something to be said for this knowing. Others came to us for it, wanting to know whether they could anchor boats in a certain bay, whether channels were deep enough for a motorboat, whether inland streams were blocked to fish passage. Sometimes botanists were stuck at a high lake and had to hike out without the floatplane that had dropped them off, and we knew the best route for them to take to salt water. It was good to know things like this. It was a way to feel like the local I would never truly be.

The water swirled around our ankles; I could feel its clammy touch seeping through my rubber boots. We stood in a bog that was a stew of decomposing plants. The bedrock at its foundation prevented water from draining off and allowed for the collection of sphagnum moss and other vegetation that formed a thick, watery sponge. On maps these were places to aim for because here you could break out of the trees and look around. We tried to stitch them together as we hiked, since the going was sometimes easier here. Sometimes, though, muskegs were a beautiful trap, our feet plunging deep into stagnant pools.

I heard what Helga said but pretended I didn't. The wind blew strong in this bay, I thought. I could easily not hear. I hadn't always been this way, I thought, shoving my water bottle back in my backpack. Had I? I could remember summer nights with the trail crew, all of us encased in layers of down, lying next to each other, easy conversation spooling out through the darkness. I hadn't had so many walls then. It seemed like my nutshell had grown slowly, imperceptibly hardening and encouraged by the years of motion, without me really knowing it was happening. Breaking free seemed almost impossible.

If there was anyone I could talk to, it was Helga. After all, we had shared so many adventures on the ocean together. We had stumbled on bears hidden deep in tall estuary grass, and we had survived heart-thumping floatplane rides when the pilot had gotten confused, or the plane had been tossed around by wind, or both. We had been stuck out because of weather and blown around on the open sea. We had picked campsites on tiny islands and hiked to trailless lakes. We had survived more together than most people ever would in a lifetime.

Yet there were still things I couldn't say. To say them made them real. To say that my marriage had foundered, that I had impulsively chosen a man based on loneliness and fear, meant that I had made a mistake I was not sure I could unravel. I was suspended the same way our feet were suspended by thick, strong layers of plants woven together in this muskeg. Out here I could look at a map and make a decision. At home, I wavered. Each option seemed fraught with danger and heartache.

"I think we can go up this way," I said, deflecting the question in her eyes. We scrambled up a set of rock ledges and fought our way through a chute, coming out next to a thin silver line of water—the lake outlet. Now

I knew we were on the right path. A waterfall, ferocious in its strength and power, catapulted past our boots and down toward the ocean in an unbroken stream. Here the going was tough, hand over hand in grass slippery as ice. A fall would have meant tumbling in an irrevocable flight. Anyone else would have turned around, but I had faith in Helga. She never turned around, not for anyone or anything. Finally, we broke over the lip of the waterfall and stood on the shore of a lake the color of slate.

In any other state this place would be swollen with people. There would be fishing trails beaten out around the shore, campsites dotted in the scarce trees. There would be trees hacked with axes and every scrap of wood gone for white man campfires, our name for the enormous blazes some people liked to build.

But not here. The lake's surface rippled gently in a shallow breeze. The far shore, at least a quarter mile away, was crowded with spiky evergreens. Unclimbed mountains rose high on both flanks. It seemed as though we were the first people to ever stand here. The gravity of where we were fell on my shoulders like stone.

We had made it, two women and an aerial photo, to a lake that fewer than a hundred people, if that, would ever visit in a year, maybe several years if it stayed a secret. We grinned at each other and high-fived.

As we approached salt water, I scanned the estuary. A few weeks earlier we had been descending a cliff just like this one, bound for our boats. A large, hulking shape had moved below, cutting us off. A bear prowled downwind, sniffing the fiberglass.

We had hunkered in the dubious safety of the forest, speaking in low whispers. "It's coming toward us!" I hissed, sure that any second, the bear would charge. With agonizing slowness, the bear finally abandoned whatever mission it was on. I let out a long, slow breath. I had lost most of my fear of the wilderness. Bears were the only one that remained.

Today no bears lingered. There was just the soft mist that by now I did not even consider rain, coating our hair and clothes in a fine spray. We went through our ritual in silence, paddling quietly toward a point that looked like wind bent around it enough to keep the white sox at bay.

You're a hard nut to crack. Was I? I remembered a moment from long ago. A man and me, sitting on another bunkhouse porch. There had been so many of these, so many times that I was leaving and someone else was staying put. "You're just like Antarctica," he had said, breaking the silence of a peaceful midwestern evening. "I love Antarctica and I know I will never get there." Then he had swung onto his bike and pedaled away.

I had dismissed his words as those of someone a few beers into the night. But was he right? Other times came back to me. The men I had left behind, adopting resigned expressions as I packed my truck. "I always knew you would leave." Others had simply vanished as my departure date had grown closer, nowhere to be found in the mountains or on the rivers. Maybe none of them had thrown a backpack in the car or asked me to stay because it had been clear to them that I would never let them below the surface.

I thought again about the trail crew and the fiction I had told myself. We had sweated over rock-hard deadfall with our crosscut saws, had scaled impossible talus slopes in search of bighorn sheep and little-visited lakes, but how well had I let them know me? In my mind there had always been the probability of moving on to the next place and the next adventure. Going it alone had seemed easier, the clean break the best path. It suddenly became clear: I had impenetrable layers of my own. My heart had always been open to the wilderness in a way it had never been for any person. My husband had become a mirror, a reflection back to myself.

I knew I could not be like that, not anymore. No matter what it took, I was going to unwrap myself from my shell. Like the scull, it would take a balance between risk and safety. I paddled after Helga, grateful for her comment.

The cliff we finally chose for our campsite was a promontory that guarded the narrow passage into the bay. Our charts told us that this had once been a native village, but no trace could be found. Tall grass parted like hair to a comb as we walked through it, setting our tents on the windiest place we could find. Below us the cliff took the full brunt of the storms. It was completely exposed to the elements, crumbling only a little under the repeated assault.

There was a couple in town who traveled, their good fortune in life meaning that they weren't tied to jobs or responsibility. They were always leaving and returning from exotic locations, claiming that home wasn't a place, but a feeling. It rested with a person, not a place. Wherever the other one was, that was home.

I wondered whether this was the right way to think about it. Maybe I had been too focused on the physical—the crunch of sand beneath my boots, the sweep of a ridge as it climbed to meet higher mountains above. Maybe home was more of an idea than that.

≈

"Can we do more things together?" I asked. I said that I was lonely. I knew that I had been gone too long; I would stay home more. Was there a movie we could watch together? Did he want to run with me the way we used to at the beginning? What about the kayak that hung on the back of the house? My husband looked baffled. "We're in the same house at the same time," he said. Wasn't that enough?

≈

He packed for a trip down south. He had applied for a job and was being flown down for an interview. He had not discussed applying for the job with me before he did it, and it was located in the kind of place he knew I hated, a soulless rush of traffic, far from any wilderness.

"What if you get it?" I asked. "There's no job there for me."

He shrugged, carefully applying polish the color of night to his dress shoes. I watched as he took a towel and blotted out the excess.

"Well," I said. Marriage was about give and take, and I had always lived my life without compromise. Maybe that was what was wrong with us. Maybe I needed to concede this one, as though marriage were a set of brief, bloody skirmishes with only one victor.

"I could give it a year," I offered. "And then if I didn't find work, we could move for me next time." That was how most Forest Service couples did it, since two good jobs in one location were rare. Sacrifice and reward; it all balanced out.

He didn't look up from his work. "I can't leave after only one year." Pause. Study the shoe. Rub in more polish. "That looks really bad."

The conversation was over. I could not believe how easily my life had been erased.

My husband started on the other shoe. It was scuffed and scarred, the leather cracked. It was hard to keep things looking good here. The one he had finished shone, perfect, as though it had never been worn.

I was learning what the lonely husbands had already known: it was possible to be more alone with someone than without. For the first time, I really understood what had propelled them out of their houses on dark winter nights, seeking reassurance that they still mattered, that they still existed.

two

Ron taxied the Beaver down the main channel to where Jesse and I stood waiting. Two inattentive kayakers off the cruise ship swerved to avoid the plane as it slowly approached the dock. Unlike some pilots who roared down the channel, scattering hapless paddlers in their wake, Ron took it nice and easy. Clients in matching yellow slickers from the fishing charters swiveled their heads as I grabbed hold of the rope Ron threw. They were wondering where we were going, two people in rain jackets with a rifle and a pile of gear.

Jesse wrestled a loaded cart down from the pickup, holding it back with all his slight frame had. The lower the tide, the steeper the ramp. This was an especially low tide and the ramp stood nearly vertical. He made it without losing any gear, though he had to break into a run to contain the cart.

Floatplanes were the taxis of Southeast Alaska. We hauled everything in them: kayaks on the floats, praying our knots held; guns and ammo; and ourselves, putting our faith in the pilots that we would make it home safely.

Jesse shifted from foot to foot, clutching his plant press. He was a botanist, more comfortable with land than air. He saw flying as a necessary evil and white-knuckled it for the entire journey. Only the hint of a rare plant would make him go airborne.

"Where we going today?" Ron asked. He hopped onto the dock, compact and rosy cheeked. He liked flying us because we got him off the main tourist routes. With us, he got to go places hardly anyone ever went.

He surveyed our mountain of gear, looking unfazed. Everybody flew like this. There was no ultralight in Southeast Alaska, where just getting wet could kill you. Somehow it all would fit, even if we sat with our legs suspended over dry bags.

Depending on where we wanted to go, it would be easy or it would be hard. If we needed to shuttle boats and people, we almost needed a diagram. That discussion went like this: One of us would fly to the bay with gear and wait. The other would remain to help Ron tie the kayaks to the floats. He would take off with the boats only, since insurance prohibited him from flying kayaks and passengers at the same time. He would drop the kayaks in the bay with the first person and then go back for the last. If all went well, nobody would be stranded and the kayaks would make it in one piece.

Today was more straightforward. We were leaving the kayaks behind and going to one of the high lakes. Ron looked almost disappointed and his expression darkened when we stated our destination. "Rust Lake," he said in tones of doom. He had taken us there before, and it was an especially tricky landing.

The pilot's word was law, and I waited uneasily for the final verdict. But Ron shrugged. "What the heck, we'll give her a try."

We flew north, flanking the steep slopes of Kruzof Island with its dormant volcano, Mount Edgecumbe, the crater a wide-mouthed bowl. To the west rose the rocky hulk of Saint Lazaria Island, a nesting bird colony where nobody but scientists were supposed to set foot. Below all that, a steady stream of watercraft headed for Vitskari Rocks and all the hidey-holes only they knew. All of this was familiar. We headed off into the unknown.

We passed over the small hollowed-out basin that held Whitestripe Lake, a location that Helga and I had visited the year before. Named for the bleached marble band that belted this wild section of Chichagof Island, this lake was remote and rarely seen. The Whitestripe marble ran like a sidewalk from high above the lake and plummeted underwater, emerging on the other side.

We had not been the first there, judging by the few scattered fire rings we found, but it had felt like we were. We had climbed through an alder thicket to reach the marble formation, thick and ropy as muscle far above the lake. Its surface was sun warmed and smooth and our rubber boots stuck to it like sandpaper. Trips to lakes like these were once in a lifetime; despite Sven's benevolent leadership, it was tough to justify more than one survey of such a little-visited place.

Soon the startling sight of a lake under siege came into view. It was unmistakably Rust Lake. Jesse hated landings more than takeoffs, and he clutched the armrests in anticipation.

"I'll try it," Ron said again. He implied that this would be an experiment that could be aborted if he felt that things were not to his liking. We made a couple of passes as he deliberated, skimming near the treetops. Finally, he dropped the plane steeply, banking into the turn, and we glided down onto the lake. We floated for a few seconds as the prop wound down and I pointed out the far end, where we needed to land.

Jesse and I trudged from plane to shore with armloads of gear, piling it onto a strange gritty sand. Ron stood on a float using an oar to keep the plane from sticking in the mud.

He grinned as he hopped back in. "See you in a couple of days!" *Maybe,* I thought. I imagined Jesse and me settling in for a winter, the lake slowly turning from an icy slush to a hardpan, using our rifle to hunt down unlucky deer, building a structure out of logs and a tarp. While I knew the chances of this were remote, my mind couldn't help creating these scenarios. I did this on the islands too, mentally cataloging the debris I could use to survive. This felt necessary in case something went wrong, but it was also tinged with a hint of desire, the desire to disappear completely.

We stood for a moment watching the plane's wake march toward shore. The lake's surface matched the sky, an uncommon blue, and winter was still far off. Any shelter building would not have to happen today.

Flying into a wilderness was not heard of elsewhere, except in some isolated situations created by legislation. The Alaska National Interest Lands Conservation Act had created fifty million acres of wilderness across the state, but not without special Alaska provisions. Point-to-point travel, much as with a taxi, was permitted here, even though it felt strange to drop from the sky in a machine and shatter the silence. If we could walk, we did, but some lakes were so armored by geography and vegetation that this was the only way. Even though I was selfishly grateful for the lift, I sometimes wondered whether we were doing the lake any favors, despite the garbage we carried out.

Before I came to Alaska, I had generally seen wilderness in black and white. It was, I knew, a place where motorized equipment and mechanical transport were essentially forbidden, a designation dreamed up by men and women who had seen the serene world they had grown up with changing irrevocably. There should, they thought, be areas where natural silence and dark skies still existed.

I had seen the places close to town where bored kids had vandalized recreation cabins, leaving spent beer cans and trash, and where adults who should have known better had left their own souvenirs: tarps, broken lawn chairs, bottles. The farther out we got, to places like this that were expensive and hard to get to, the fewer traces of people we found.

The obvious inference was to keep people out at all costs, the credo most wilderness managers lived by, but I wondered. If I could bring people to the places I had been, how long would it take before they realized how important wilderness was? A night in a tent, with wild creatures prowling through the forest? Weeks, months of smelling spruce needles after rain, watching a storm petrel glide across the ocean? I thought that wilderness seeped into people slowly, like mist. Soon they would know they needed the silence, the mystery, the contrast to what was already known.

Jesse and I stood on the shore of the lake watching the floatplane taxi across the lake in an explosion of sound. A Beaver floatplane had an unmistakable growl, a piercing windup to departure. I thought that all the creatures nearby must be cowering from the unexpected sound. The silence seemed deeper than usual once the plane diminished to a dot in the sky. What was left was only the gurgle of water from the inlet, loud in the sudden quiet.

"Remember last time?" I asked Jesse. We had come with a group of three others on what had been meant to be a day trip. It was a Friday, right before the weekend, and we should have known better. You never planned a work trip on Fridays.

Armed with a rifle and an inflatable boat, we were looking at how to free the lake by unblocking its historic outlet. As we had gathered up our gear at the end of the day, an ominous fog had loomed over the surrounding mountains and marched toward us, enveloping us completely. Overhead we heard the plane circling fruitlessly in an attempt to find a sucker hole.

"Have a good night, folks," the pilot's voice had crackled over our radio, and there it was: stuck out again.

I was left with four men who had brought no survival supplies and little food. If they went out, they went by motorboat, not on foot or by plane, and being stuck had always been because of worsening seas. In those circumstances, they had been able to anchor up and sleep aboard, not hunker down through a night without shelter.

Expecting the worst, I had hauled in a tent, sleeping bag, and firefighter meals, sawdust-tasting blocks of largely unidentified rations. Sven had looked askance at the massif of gear I had shown up with, but now he gazed at my tent with longing. It was a two person and I had the sinking feeling I would not be bunking alone.

One of the men foraged in the woods and returned with a handful of bright orange fungus. "Chicken of the woods," he explained. "It's edible."

Just barely, was the consensus. The men huddled close to the fire, scheming ways of escape. Nobody slept much, wrapped around coals as best they could. As I had predicted, Sven shared my tent, sleeping on our life vests and snoring happily.

The next morning, fog still hung around the lake like an uninvited guest. It trailed like long skirts down to the water, teasing us by lifting briefly to show the hidden mountains.

The men paced. Talk turned to walking to salt water, an endeavor that theoretically could be done. In the old days, miners had forged a path from sea to lake to build the pipeline. I knew that traces of the old path could still be found if you looked hard enough. But most of it had been swallowed up by time and vegetation. It would be easy to slip off a hidden cliff, or to wander far from the easier way and end up rimmed out on rocks that were unclimbable. Without a map, it seemed unsafe to venture out into the unknown.

We gnawed on what was left of our food and speculated about our future. We had no way of knowing what the conditions were like far below. The ocean could be encased in the same fog that we were. A rescue mission could take a whole day to reach the estuary. It made sense to stay put, I argued.

The men grumbled. It was Saturday, they complained. Someone had a flight to Juneau the next day he could not miss. Another commandeered the satellite phone and stomped the shore making expensive calls. When a break in the weather allowed the plane to slip in and retrieve us, they cheered. They had, they implied, survived a dangerous and uncertain fate.

I laughed, remembering the eagerness to board the plane, as if we had only seconds to spare. As Jesse and I readied our day packs, I remembered one other time the two of us had been stuck out. The outer coast we had to traverse to reach White Sulphur Springs was rough and dangerous, so we had opted for a souped-up Cessna ride into a lake so small that, leaving, the pilot nearly clipped the trees on the opposite side. Jesse paled at the sight and eyed the radio, contemplating a boat pickup instead. On the day we were to leave, the plane circled for a few minutes and did not land.

Because the lake was so small, the wind had to be just right, and it wasn't, the pilot informed us curtly. We would just have to stay, and maybe tomorrow would be better.

Jesse and I looked at each other with dawning glee. We had won the jackpot this time. Not only were we able to stay in a nearby recreation cabin, complete with bunks and a roof, but there was a hot spring pool a few steps away. We could float weightless in the pool and open the large sliding glass window of the shelter that contained it to see surf pound the coast below us. To top it off, one of the last cabin visitors had left a box of wine in the outdoor cooler box. Nobody would believe this, we thought, deciding to leave out the wine part of the story.

If we got stuck out this time, I thought, it wouldn't be the end of the world. There were worse places to be, like at our desks staring at computer screens. Then Jesse reminded me of his bear story. With another botanist, he had sat right where we were now, watching a deer drink from the lake on the other side of the inlet.

Jesse was an unhurried guy and he finished the story in his own time. While they watched the bucolic nature scene, a bear had sneaked out of the forest and dragged the deer away. He shrugged, unfazed. Bears, unlike flying, did not bother Jesse.

Rust Lake was a disagreeable spot, a sore thumb in the middle of the wilderness. Decades ago, miners had trudged a treacherous route from salt water, carrying dynamite and shovels, to dig a long tunnel to tap the lake for hydroelectric power for a mine the next bay over. We had seen the remains of both the hydro plant and the mine, both defunct years ago, but the tap still existed, slowly lowering the lake's water level below what it would naturally have been. Today our landing had been touch and go since a drier than usual summer had kept the replenishing rains away. Because of this, a bathtub ring lined the lake with silty, coarse sand where the waterline should be.

We had found the valve that controlled the tap, rusted open. Something was blocking the tunnel, but how to clear it? Anyone diving into it could be sucked in by the powerful force of pent-up water at the edge of the tunnel.

Jesse looked doubtfully at the old channel, the original outlet when the lake had been free. It had been plugged up for decades, and a new forest had taken hold. Releasing the volume of water that now flowed through the tunnel would create a tidal wave, a torrent of mud and water that would roll over this landscape, uprooting trees and carrying sediment far below. Maybe it would be better to leave it alone. The damage had already been done.

The last time he had been here, the time with the bear, Jesse and the other botanist had climbed high above the lake to a limestone outcrop. Caves pockmarked the rock, and places like this were where rare plants were sometimes found. On their way back, they had discovered a strange poppy, one they had not seen before. It could, Jesse told me, be a new species. He had determined to come back and check.

This was what I liked about Southeast Alaska. There were mysteries in the mountains. So few feet had trodden the interior that you never knew what was back there, waiting to be found. Up on the blush-colored cliffs near Red Bluff Bay, a pair of different botanists had documented plants that grew only in ultramafic rock. They had shown me how compasses spun wildly because of the iron in the strange outcrop. One other time a guide showed me a grave he had found, mutely sitting out the years on an unremarkable bluff. He had found it when his heel scraped away decades' worth of moss. Here it always felt like the next discovery was minutes away.

I was always up for a treasure hunt and, forsaking my kayak, had invited myself along for this land-based adventure. Discouraged by constant rain and the possibility of being stuck out, any coworkers who could have edged me out of the trip, people with actual botanical knowledge, had declined, preferring a roof over their heads. I couldn't believe my luck.

After stashing our gear in what I fervently hoped was a bear-free zone, we hiked up a gash in the land where the inlet poured into the lake. I conceded the rifle to Jesse, glad to be shed of the weight and the responsibility. The depth of the draw that water had scoured over years showed the free fall of rain and snowmelt that constantly collided with the land. I had heard that water poured off this island in measurements of feet per year, and this was evident by the ravaged landscape we walked through.

"Here they are," Jesse said.

"What?" I asked. Bears? Did he mean bears?

"The *poppies*," Jesse said. He pointed to a cluster of spindly-stemmed plants waving bravely in the chilly air. "This is what we're looking for," he said.

I bent for a closer look, my fear of bears forgotten. The flowers, curved upward like the palm of a hand, were the color of sunshine. They seemed out of place in the gray and dull green landscape, as if someone had scattered pieces of gold across the gravel.

The poppies, Jesse said, grew in inhospitable places. They didn't take it easy. They liked gravel washes, spots where a torrent of water had raked the soil bare, where survival was uncertain at best. The following year Jesse would come back and find that this population had disappeared under layers of rock deposited from winter rains. When he told me this, I sighed, but Jesse just shrugged. That was the way it was in the botanical world. Survival of the fittest. The plants might come back another year, or they might not. There was nothing we could do about it.

Jesse shot up a vertical slope like a rocket and I struggled to gain purchase in gravel that slid me back with every step. "This is extreme botany," I panted as we hopped the inlet and headed up the mouth of the wash. We were hiking straight up, no switchbacks, the trees left behind a couple of hundred feet ago. Old snow crusted the peaks around us. Below, the lake was a blue bowl, looking almost beautiful. The bears, if there were any, remained unseen.

"Here's some!" I exclaimed, finding a cluster of poppies in a random spot. We found a few other scatterings, gradually giving way to a barren hillside.

Poppies grew in places like this where the earth was reinventing itself. They were colonizers, venturing out into barren ground that was too desperate for other, less hardy plants. Once they had lived and died, their remains paved the way for a new ecosystem to take hold.

"Do you think these are really a new species?" I pestered Jesse. I wanted them to be.

"Don't know," he said. "Maybe." He didn't seem invested in the outcome.

I knew poppies were not Jesse's first love. Like most botanists, he lusted after the small and secretive: moonworts or the small mosses that clung desperately to life in the spray zones of waterfalls. The poppies were brash and in your face. Even I, a hopeless student of plants, could see them.

I stole a glance at the poppies as we descended back to camp. Jesse collected a plant to encase in his press and send off to a lab in Norway for the final answer. I knew that botanists did not endow the plants they studied with human qualities, but as I saw them, all I could think of was brave.

three

"Don't lift the pot lid on the rice!" Andy hollered. Helga dropped the lid with a clatter. Avoiding each other's eyes, we tried not to snicker. Even out here in the wilderness, some people lived and died by the same rules they followed in town. To me, this was the perfect occasion to be lawless: paddle after dark, skinny-dip, peek at cooking rice.

From our campsite on a petite island, I scanned the adjacent mainland. It was the height of salmon season, and bears trudged back and forth from day beds to river in a constant parade. The smell of rotting fish reached us even across the water, and the occasional corpse washed up on our beach. Darkness was slowly overtaking us, the light still lingering on top of the highest peaks, the river valleys in deep shadow. It was a spooky time, the transition between night and day.

Obediently, Helga and I watched the cook pot without budging, looking for the telltale bubble of smoke that would signal boiling. When we saw it, I turned down our WhisperLite stove to what passed for a simmer. Andy sat beside us on a stump, glowering, no doubt regretting his decision to accompany us and our irreverent style of cooking.

The three of us were on a mission to locate a possible new trail to a recreation cabin. The old one was deemed too close to the river, portions of it flooding out every year. There were also rumors of an outlaw cabin on this island, and we had determined to search every inch until we found it.

This island and its smaller cousin nearby had been hard hit by a human-caused wildfire years before. Ghostly silver snags rose silently from the tangle of brush that covered most of the island. The whole landscape felt forlorn and desolate, but still magical in its remoteness.

A salmon troller passed by in the strait, downriggers high in the air. It was headed for shelter farther up the coast, our small camp completely unnoticed. I could hear the faint thump of bass as it passed, the crew jamming out to hard rock.

We settled down on the beach with our plates of food. The rice had turned out perfectly, despite our egregious mistake. Spreading charts and topo maps over our laps, we discussed the next day's plan.

Unlike Helga and me, Andy wasn't crazy about staying out overnight. If it had been up to us, we would have stayed out all summer, seldom going to town. We were alike that way. But most people got their dose of wilderness in small shots and then were ready to go home.

They might have had happier homes to go back to, I thought, filling up a pot with water for dishes. By now, mine felt as barren as the places where the fire had been. In contrast, the wilderness was alive. As I waited for the water to heat, I could see three bears snuffling along the shoreline opposite us. A raft of sea otters floated offshore, grasping their dinner of sea urchins. Somewhere out there, unseen, I knew whales swam. In my few years paddling these coasts, I had seen only a tiny fraction of what existed.

Of course, we couldn't see it all. Chichagof Island's coastline measured over seven hundred miles, and Baranof's was about a hundred more, if you counted all the indentations and dips in the shoreline. Nobody could do it all in a season; the intrepid souls who had circumnavigated the islands had been forced to adopt straighter lines. Instead, we had to pick the places where people went—the hunters, the outfitters, the sightseers—and also some of the places they didn't, to make sure the wilderness stayed the way it was.

Even as we explored, I knew we were documenting a place that had been shaped by people. First there were the Tlingit and the Haida, living in harmony with tide and forest, driven out by the Russians in bloody battles. The invaders cut down trees to feed their furnaces, the enormous stumps still visible. They forced Aleut hunters to go after otters and seals, redesigning kayaks so they could fit three paddlers.

Finally, there were the miners and settlers, hunting for gold or whatever the forest could give them. Once there were more people living on both coasts than there were now, hundreds of them scraping out a living in a place where it rained more than six feet a year. You could not separate the people from the wilderness. They were braided together.

But the wilderness was growing back. We saw that evidence as we hiked the trail the next day, noting places where it was no longer sustainable. It was the same problem everywhere. Boardwalks warped and rotted under the constant pressure of the rain. Surfaces that remained were slippery to the point of being uncrossable. Water pooled in enormous puddles in other places, the tourists sidestepping them until the trail tread widened far into the forest or turned into a mud-sucking bog. Bridges were swallowed by rain-swollen streams. Rivers changed course, flooding paths, and landslides and avalanches overtook recreation cabins, eliminating them completely. It was a constant battle.

Our crew of three could do little to stem the other changes that were coming. Not only were more people in more boats clogging the bays, fishing out the halibut and herring, but an unseen menace was warming the climate. The old snows were a thing of the past. In town, we even heard the boom of thunder, electrical storms a recent phenomenon in this maritime climate. Cedar trees were dying in massive numbers, killed by the lack of insulating snow in winter. There were people who clung stubbornly to the belief that this place would never change. It was too wild, too wet, too many bears, they claimed. Those of us on the coasts in small boats knew better.

On the trail the next day, we interrupted a feeding frenzy. Our boots tracked through a stew of slime and blood and bear piss. Salmon corpses were flung onto the rocks, some chewed in half by recent teeth. The bears could afford to be choosy and they had been, ripping out the stomachs and leaving the rest. The stink of rotting fish was a slow burn in my nostrils and I took careful steps, feeling a legion of eyes on me from the dark forest.

We were crossing the tidal slough when we saw him. He was moving slowly down the stream, a deep chocolate brown, the ends of his fur silver with rain. I had seen many bears, but I had never been this close.

Everything worked the way it was supposed to, the way Moe had taught us. Pull back the action to jack the ammo into the chamber. Stand tall and yell. Convince the bear that he did not want to mess with us.

There was one moment when it could have gone either way. The bear stopped and looked at us, moving his head from side to side. He turned broadside to show us he was a big, bad dude. Everything boiled down to the hushed essence of mutual recognition, with the soft rain dripping down our faces and the fog sliding through the trees. What was probably only a few seconds felt like much longer.

It was almost as if the bear had decided we were not worth the bother. He stared at us a moment longer, then turned and ambled slowly into the woods. Though he was probably not very far off the trail, he had utterly vanished.

≈

We gained the safety of the cabin, having determined no better path. Anything else would still carve a swath through the ancient forest, changing the way the water drained through the soil and moving the bears out when people walked on it. It was hard to balance their desire against keeping it wild. Sometimes it seemed that we beat against an invisible current, going nowhere.

On the boardwalk heading back to our boats, I searched for the bear. Surely it had drifted somewhere back in the forest, watching us. On alert, we skirted the estuary and crossed the place where it flooded at high tide. Today it was placid at slack and we could jump across without taking off our boots. Though the estuary teemed with life, with all the small creatures that lived in a constant state of dry and wet, there were no bears to be seen. I knew that after we passed through, and the swirl of water and mud made by our footprints settled back into stillness, they would return. This was their place, not ours.

ferry

A kayak instructor will tell you that a ferry stroke involves angling the boat to move sideways or upstream against a current. What they may not say is that a ferry is a way to trick the water.

It is a shortcut, a sneak. You use it when you want to go somewhere that the ocean doesn't want you to go. You might think that if you want to move from the fish weir to an island across the channel, an island that you hope the bears will ignore because it is so small, you simply point the bow of your boat in that direction. In anything other than calm water, you would be wrong. If you are in a bay that empties its guts out into the strait twice daily, you need to start at an angle and stick to it, even when it looks like you are going the wrong way.

You have to keep the end goal in mind when ferrying. This is where patience pays off. If you give up halfway across, you could lose momentum and be swept to a place of disaster: sharp-toothed rocks, surf, spat out the entrance of a bay. A ferry requires the ability to plan ahead. It is not for those who operate on a wing and a prayer.

one

We ferried toward an unnamed island, fighting the inbound tide. The island was our only hope for camping; it was the last one before we would be swept out to the main channel. The fish weir guys across the bay watched impassively, perhaps wondering why we were willingly committing ourselves to the predicted gales. They had a cabin to retreat to, a plywood shack perched on a ledge above the river. Down by the water, they had rigged up a solar shower. They lived out here for weeks at a time, turning almost feral. I wasn't exactly sure what they did all day, but they weren't going to tell us. When we arrived, we tried to talk with them, but they were nearly silent. They had nothing to say to us.

I glanced over at Helga, doing her own ferry, but I knew she couldn't help me. We were each locked in our own private battle against the elements. In a single kayak you couldn't do much to save the other. Even though we paddled in parallel lines, we were each on our own.

I dug in with my paddle, aiming for a point far above the island's tip. There was no use in fighting the ocean. Instead, I tried to find weaknesses in it. We could break the current by pointing our boats perpendicular to it, by fooling it into thinking we were headed in a different direction.

Though I knew the ocean was not a living thing, it often seemed that way. I imagined I could hear its impatient breath in the sigh of an incoming tide. The push of waves that helped us beach our boats was a helping hand at my back. Other times the ocean appeared angry, the roar of the swell breaking in a froth of teeth on the cliffs. From time to time it was steeped in despair, fog reaching down to the silver surface, an indolent swell slowly lifting our boats.

Sometimes the ocean's moods matched mine: a sparkly, spunky surf, a misty rain close to tears. Though I knew that this was not the way most Alaskans saw the sea, it was hard not to personalize it. I spent so much time with it that the ocean became a fickle companion, playful yet not to be trusted.

We shared information up and down the coast. The guides, calling in on satellite phones, told me about early ice on the bay surfaces. The pilots on the float dock reported wind shears raking the outside passages, storms gathering strength over the straits. Commercial fishermen told about new landslides gouged out of the belly of a mountain. From one end of town to the other, we gauged how thick the clouds, how heavy the rain. Still, the weather was often a mystery. I sometimes backed out of a patrol because of an ominous forecast, only to be surprised by calm seas. Other times I went for it, and we were pinned down on a tiny island by pounding surf.

On some of the lakes, the day could dawn hard bright, but if the wind was off slightly, the pilot would overfly and not be able to land. Other times a plane dropped out of a lowering sky like a bullet when I was certain we would be left behind.

In the end I had to give up and accept what came. We huddled over the radio listening to the automated voice passionlessly report the forecast. It was for a wide area, though, and there could be isolated pockets of sunshine or storm. You could sit all day on the beach because of a bad forecast, and all day the water would remain playful and easy. Other times you went for it and were horrified by the mistake you had made.

. After several minutes of ferrying, we gained the island. It was a poor spot for a camp, dark and sodden, leftover rain dripping from the trees. It would be a hard ferry to anywhere else, and too late to try. We set to work, spooling out a long line of parachute cord and knotting it to two trees. Over that we unfolded a tarp, securing the grommets to more lines branching out from limbs. We set up our tents under the tarp, leaving enough space for a front porch where we could leave soaked rain gear or change clothes.

We had done this so many times that I was feeling accomplished as I turned to unpack my personal gear. It was then that I noticed with horror that I had forgotten the one most essential item: a sleeping bag.

Sometimes on the coldest of patrols, those where I blew into my fingers to feel some heat, when rain pestered its way through the dry suit and under my ball cap, all I dreamed about was the end of the day, when I could shuck my wet clothes, pull on dry ones, and slide into my bag. It was like a hug made of feathers. To have forgotten it was a disaster.

I couldn't call the floatplane to bring it to me; this would be a $1,000 flight. I refused to bail out early, sabotaging our patrol. Nobody did that.

"You can snuggle with me," Helga said, but my pride wouldn't let me. I would make it work, I resolved.

For all of the five days, it rained hard. The temperature refused to budge past forty degrees. We were out in the downpour all day, bent over our clipboards as we sketched campsite layouts and recorded each boat we saw. Every night I crawled into my tent with optimism. It wouldn't really be that bad. The first night I rolled up in a large blue tarp. This was a big mistake, as I was covered in condensation the next morning. The next night I put on all the clothes I had: fleece pants, long underwear, dry suit. It wasn't enough. For each of the five miserable, unendurable nights, I shivered awake, regretting my folly in not checking everything the night before leaving. It was a mistake I would never make again. This was how you learned the importance of shelter. A mistake like this could straddle the thin line between survival and safety, going either way.

Shelters were the most important to us, but after we established our tent sites, the next most important structure was the kitchen tarp, farther away down the beach in case bears decided to investigate. We sank our bear canister of perishable food halfway into the water, with a rock on top so it would not float away in the tide. We hung the remaining food bag in the trees, fifteen feet high and six feet out from the tree trunk. Although the bears had plenty of salmon to rely on, it was better not to take chances with our bagels and cheese. If our food was taken, it would be a hungry wait for a ride that might not make it for several days.

Camp chores done, we retrieved the boats, lighter now, and set off into the bay to conduct our patrol. This bay, several miles deep and hundreds of feet wide, had been home to many people when the Hirst-Chichagof silver and gold mine had been operating. The mine had run for twenty-four hours a day in the 1930s, pausing only on Christmas Day. A large tailings pile was slowly leaching into the sea, and as we pushed through the alders, we found remains of houses, doorless and windowless to the rain.

As we tramped through the remains of the village, we made up stories about what each had been. This long, rectangular building must have been the dance hall. This one, a schoolhouse. An old wooden barge lay at the water's edge, and above the houses, rails led back into a mine tunnel. The forest was slowly taking it all over.

Done with our exploration, pictures taken for the archaeologist, we rode a fresh tide into Lake Anna. Really a saltwater lake, its only entrance was a slim passage that restricted boat traffic at flood. The remains of a powerhouse, the conduit that kept the Chichagof mine running, guarded a point near the outlet. A lone bear paused in its foraging and stared at us. "This makes seven," Helga said; she had been keeping a running tally. We would later report back to the wildlife biologist.

The bears were on the move. We saw them in the estuaries, seven strong, grazing like cows on the sedges. They splashed through the salmon streams, leaving half-eaten carcasses rotting on the banks. They ambled away from us as we walked through the forest with clipboards searching for campsites and weeds to inventory.

We sang as we walked, off-key renditions of songs we half remembered. "Hey, bear!" we shouted, our voices echoing through the forest. My coworkers returned from the field with stories that reinforced my fear: a bear, unseen, emitting deep growls below them; a charge and a shot fired, a rifle jammed, a bear shot to save their lives. Sometimes a bear was just having a bad day.

I was afraid of bears, a fear that went beyond the reasonable. For years bears had haunted my dreams, hunting me down. I imagined them lurking behind every spruce, every alder patch, waiting to jump out as I passed.

At first, I thought camping on islands would be safe. That was before I saw bears industriously swimming between islands. They went everywhere. There were no boundaries for bears.

Chichagof Island had a higher population of brown bears per square mile than anywhere else on earth. There was no disputing this when we saw evidence every day. Helga and I hiked quickly through tall grass, coming upon day beds recently vacated, bare patches of ground still holding the outline of a recent occupant. "The bear outhouse," she commented as we found enormous, coal-black piles of scat. We saw where bears had raked up skunk cabbage with their claws or tested logs for grubs. Bears gnawed on our trail signs and on doors of the recreation cabins. Even when we didn't see them, I felt their solid presence.

Helga lay down in a bear trail, sticking her hands in the tracks to show me how large the walkers had been. Generations of bears—mothers, fathers, grandfathers—had walked in each other's footprints, pressing their toes hard into the spongy earth. Over years, these tracks set up like plaster on the forest floor. We followed them as far as we dared, marveling at the depth and size of the tracks. These bear trails meandered through every inch of the forest, bear highways between day beds, streams, and estuary.

"Let's get out of here," I said, spooked. We returned to our boats and paralleled the shore. Though these looked like islands, I reminded myself that we were actually paddling past the tops of a submerged mountain range. Their bases extended far beyond where we could see or breathe. There were hundreds of these sunken mountains, plunging to the ocean floor, taller than Everest.

Our paddles pushed through the delightfully named "sunlit zone" of the ocean, the uppermost layer of a series of five. Like tiers of a cake, these layers descended to the deepest zone of all, the one where no light ever reached. These layers were demarcated by the presence of light, not depth; here the sunlit zone stretched down over hundreds of feet.

Sometimes, when the cold breath of the ocean stirred beneath me, I thought about all those zones below my boat, unseen and unknown. Because there were hours in which to think, hours during which we paddled together but separately, my mind wandered in giant circles, dreaming up the ways the ocean and people were similar. In the place the scientists called the abyss, there was perpetual darkness. Only a few strange creatures lived there, surviving mostly on food that fell like rain from layers above. This, I thought in times when my mind roamed in fanciful bursts, was the bottom of the soul, the darkness in all of us.

two

I never liked the way we killed halibut. Whenever we pulled one out of the water, its lungs a bellows on the slippery floor of the boat, I turned away as my husband hit it with the bat. Blood ran over our rubber boots, blood that we washed away with the hose back at the docks. I watched it stream diluted back into the sea along with the pieces of fish that we didn't want. Sea lions swam as close as they dared for our castoffs. The smell of blood mixed with the salt and the fish, a dank cloud I could almost taste.

Other people shot halibut instead of using a hook or a bat. Small-arms fire peppered the air out at the fishing grounds of Vitskari Rocks. You got used to it. You could get used to anything, even the continuous rain that filtered from the sky without ceasing. You got used to the way the halibut came up to the surface on your line, mystical flat fish with huge eyes. You got used to beauty and killing, all in one moment.

We ate the fish silently in our house, the television on to fill the gaps in our conversation. By now, three years into Alaska, I could tell the differences in the fish we caught: rich king salmon, oily on my tongue; flavorful rockfish, shunned by some as bottom feeders; and halibut, flaky white flesh, so easy to overcook.

We had run out of things to say to each other in the first year of marriage. So we went fishing. That was about the only thing we still did together, because we needed to, because we wanted the food. There was always something to do on the boat. Drive slowly in a spiral, watching out for other boats. Stand poised by the downriggers, ready to reel them in if the bottom got too shallow or one of them bent enough to mean a fish or a snag. Untangle lines. Rebait the hooks. Fishing kept us from thinking too much.

Before this, I had strictly adhered to catch and release, knee deep in a trout stream. Men had taught me to fly-fish in the Yellowstone and in creeks that drained out of the mountains, but I liked to fish alone, the line curling over my head a meditation. I rarely caught fish, but I didn't care. I didn't want to eat the slender cutthroats that darted from pools as I approached, ungainly in my waders. I wanted instead to see the dance between line and water. I wanted to watch as my cast curled gently into the current and the fly disappeared. When I actually caught a fish, I was torn between elation and guilt. I knelt by the bank, hurrying, holding my breath until it wriggled away.

In Alaska, we fished for food. Everyone did it, loading up their boats with dipping nets and heading for Redoubt Bay to pull in their quotas. They steamed out before dawn for the secret and not-so-secret hidey-holes, watching the tides to be there at the precise moment of turn. We were all overcome with fish lust, harvesting way more than we could eat in one season. We jockeyed for space with the other boats, locals and guides alike, the latter carrying the people we called pukers, mostly hefty older men in yellow ponchos from states like Texas, New York.

We spoke in secret code to our friends on other boats, trying to ascertain their luck. Out here, though, it was each boat for itself. My husband and I were our own world, the other boats passing close enough to touch, but separate. Out here on the ocean, someone might throw you a line if you needed it, but you were expected to be self-reliant and strong. It was the same on land. Living on an island, you didn't broadcast your problems. You went about your own business. You didn't talk about how this marriage made you feel so alone that you wanted to slip into the icy water just like a fish, swim deep, deep under and never surface.

When we came back in to the dock, others nodded at the cleaning station. Gulls punctured the choppy water. Floatplanes buzzed by in a spray of water, taking people to the other small villages down the coast. Our hands freezing, salt water stinging the cracks the wind and rain made, we hurried the job of filleting, each fish something to stack against hunger and long winters when the gales made us stay close to shore.

As we docked the boat into its slip and I wound the line around the cleat, I thought about all the things I would do differently if I dared. Keep only a few fish. Let the old ones return to the water, the ones eighty, one hundred years old. Find my own boat and go my own way.

Instead I wiped bloody hands on my rain pants. There was still work to do. We had to vacuum seal our fish and set them to chill into frozen blocks in the freezer. Days, weeks, months, maybe years from now we would pull them out to thaw and eat, the taste of rain, wind, salt and regret mingled together on our lips.

three

In Southeast Alaska, there were two kinds of people: the ones who had always been there, and the ones who had chosen it. The others, the ones who gave it a try and decided this place wasn't for them, left as soon as they could. This wasn't like the other places I had lived, where you could cultivate a deep indifference to place but stay there anyway. There had been many people like this in other towns, people who moved from one enclosed space to another, brushing up against the landscape as seldom as possible. Here, you were absorbed into the land as part of its fabric. The weather, the length of daylight, and the sea dictated nearly every move.

The ones who had chosen Alaska intrigued me, because this was what I was trying to learn. What was it about a piece of ground that captured someone? What were the reasons that someone decided that out of all the places in the world, this was the one that mattered? I had passed through remote and wild landscapes, but none of them had stuck. I wanted to be as certain as these people were. What was the secret?

These men and women moved easily through land and sea. They had adopted the language of boats and tides even if they had come from flat, inland states. "This is my homeland," Captain Johnny said as he ferried us to an isolated point in the Myriads, spinning the wheel of his boat with one hand, even though I knew he had been born elsewhere.

"Don't you miss the sun?" I asked him and the others who said this. "Wearing shorts? Road trips?"

They stared at me with incomprehension and listed their reasons: Pulling a winter king salmon from the water and grilling it the same day, the taste incomparable to the plastic-encased supermarket fish much of the rest of the country had to endure. The wild and mysterious ocean. How life here was lived on the edge, bears and people and wilderness, where you could feel truly alive. For this, they would tolerate the relative lack of fresh vegetables, the slow barge up from the south, the absence of sun.

"When the sun comes out, this is the most beautiful place in the world," Captain Johnny said, and I thought he was right. For weeks we went about our lives feeling the presence of the peaks above us, but they were shrouded in clouds. When the sun won a brief battle against the rain and the mountains showed up, you still stared like a tourist, unbelieving. It was impossible, you would think, for them to be real.

I had always thought that once I rounded that last corner, found the one place I was meant to be, life would cease to be a difficult ferry. I had also thought that paddling a kayak meant a smooth glide through the ocean, not a battle of wits and aching muscles to beat an incoming tide and a swell from the unbroken sea. I was finding out I was wrong.

≈

In a kayak, during the quarter or the ferry, I worked the rudder, setting my feet on two pegs inside the cockpit. Depending on which one I pressed, the rudder swiveled to slice through the water at the angle I needed. Some paddlers eschewed the rudder, saying that to become truly skilled you had to learn to stroke without it. It was a crutch, they said, and you never really learned your boat until you were able to control it with just your body and wits.

They were probably right, but I needed to use all the tools I had. Crossing mountain rivers, there was the right way and the wrong way. In a river swollen with snowmelt, you ferried your way to the other side, breaking the current, leaning on a makeshift wooden stick. The people who died were the ones who charged the water head on in a straight line. It was the same with the sea. What you couldn't fight, you worked around.

Helga and I flew to the other side of the island in winter, on our days off, eager to spend more days in a place we were usually forced to pass through quickly. We landed in open water at a small outpost with only three year-round residents. The summer homes here, small wooden structures, were connected by a long boardwalk, and we stayed in one of those, having the good fortune to know someone who owned it.

The water had been shut off and drained, so we had to haul buckets from the sea to flush the toilet. There were no showers, but there were hot springs pools where we rested our arms on steaming black rocks, submerged entirely but for our heads, our hair sculpted like frosty flowers.

During the afternoons we copied the bears, setting ourselves up in day beds on the long sofas. Later, when slothfulness became too much to bear, we ventured out to climb in snowshoes to a frozen lake. We slid in our boots along the flat surface, swept clean by wind. Helga rushed a hill and jumped off it in her snowshoes, flipping into deep snow. "Do it again!" I urged, captivated by her leap into blue sky. We mixed Baileys into our hot chocolate and ate without regard for calories. My inner voice was completely, blissfully silent.

On those long winter afternoons, when the sun hit the house for only fifteen minutes before retreating to the other side of the bay, I began to tell her about how difficult I was finding it to navigate my marriage. How I did not have the tools, but they had to be there somewhere. There had to be a way, I said, to slip through the current; I was exhausting myself trying to steam ahead, rudderless.

Helga listened without censure. I had to either quit or figure out how to keep going, she said. Just make a decision and stick with it, the way I was able to on the ocean. I was Gertrude out there; I could be Gertrude on land. She had ferried with me on difficult passages. She knew sometimes that was the only way.

As we lay in our day beds, the blue light of late winter lying heavy on the snow outside, I began to remember what it had been like to be alone. Not the loneliness that had seared through me, as fierce as lightning, on the empty street as a lonely, rejected husband trudged home. Instead, there had also been moments when I had curled up under a blanket the way I was now, steaming mug in hand, an entire delicious solitary afternoon stretching out before me. Choices made from loneliness were desperate ones, much like when a paddler chose to stay in the boat despite a deteriorating sea. The parallel lives my husband and I now lived were lonelier than any night on a deserted street.

My friend and I stayed up late, the wood stove glowing a cherry red, the windows fogged with our breath. We talked about the roads our lives had taken to get to this place, our hands cupped around steaming mugs. Helga had followed a man to Alaska and sometimes questioned the line between love and independence. It seemed thin to both of us, with chasms on either side. Slowly, what was knotted up inside me began to unravel.

After years of being silent, I was learning how to speak. Helga was becoming more than just my ocean friend. She was becoming the first real friend I had had in years, the first person I had let below the surface of my sea. She had seen the mistakes I had made, both on land and on the water. She would shake her head, but she would also smile. It was a revelation.

I had tried this with my husband, but he refused to venture into the less hospitable, uncertain depths. There you could run out of air. You could see things that frightened you. He always retreated back to the sunlit layer, the one that most people showed the world. There were times I couldn't blame him. Why not choose the easy route instead of the ferry? Strokes like these were why beginners settled for calm, wind-free lakes to paddle, or gave it up completely. The risk wasn't worth the reward sometimes.

Helga and I boarded the floatplane for home, captained by a gruff old-timer who disparaged the government as he waited for us to stow away our dry bags. The plane lifted off the bay and I looked back at the small outpost, wooden buildings standing defiantly despite the constant blast from wind and rain. The ferry was teaching me what was possible if you persevered. Often during a difficult ferry, I felt like giving up. I looked back at the relative safety of where I had been. Surely it would be simpler to stop beating against the tide and waves. But I had given up before, and I refused to do it again. There was an outline of a distant island ahead, one I had always wanted to reach. Just a few more ferry strokes and I would be there.

brace

If you entrust yourself to the water in a small boat, you must nail the brace. There are two kinds, one for times of mild concern, the other for more extreme situations. Above all, the braces are used when you feel unbalanced. They give you stability, or at least the illusion of it. Ultimately, the braces are a recovery stroke. They protect you from danger. Knowing when to do a brace can save your life.

The high brace can right you even when your boat is lying on a desperate edge. The main components are vertical forearms and a hefty slap of the blade onto the water's surface, but the paddle alone can't save you. Instead, your body must roll up at the same time, pulling up with the knee closest to the water and keeping your head low, the last thing to rise.

The low brace is similar and is called this because your paddle is kept at a low angle during the stroke. It should be the first line of defense against a capsize. If you are lucky, a low brace will be all you need to regain your balance.

You must practice these until you do them without thinking. Your body retains the muscle memory and you will find that bracing is instinctual, a survival mechanism.

one

My husband left for a goat hunting trip. He swung his bags onto the float-plane without a backward glance. I knew he was glad to be going, off to a wilderness lake where he could do what he wanted without the emotional tug-of-war we fought daily. He was always happiest when left alone, and there were times I imagined he wanted to be free, too, although he had never said so.

The forecast called for rain and lots of it, but he whistled, unconcerned, ready to be on his way. The pilot fired up the engine and both men faced forward, ready to go. Watching the plane leave, I felt a pang of regret and sorrow. There was a glimpse of the man I had thought I loved in the smile he gave the pilot as the plane left the runway. My heart twisted. I hadn't seen that smile in a long time. What had happened to us?

There was no one place that I could see where it had gone wrong, where we had lost our way. At some point we had failed to follow our compasses. Tiny cracks had appeared in our marriage and we had not moved to fix them. We had once both geared up to walk the dog, pulling on rubber boots and raincoats and headlamps, and now we went out separately while the other one stayed home. We had gone for long runs together, and now we went alone. The answer, I knew, was that we had looked right past each other. The man and woman we had been at the beginning were the same ones we were now. We had just refused to see it.

While he was gone, I flew in a helicopter with a biologist, looking for goats. We were not looking to shoot them, only to count them. Mountain goats had been introduced to the island years before, quickly taking hold, and the botanists hated them. The goats wallowed with unconcern among rare plants; they dug up fragile tundra. Many would say they did not belong.

But I liked seeing them, their fur not the color of snow like I had pictured but a yellow-tinged hue that stood out on the slate cliffs. They climbed to inhospitable places, living out their lives in brutal rain and snow. Sometimes they took a leap of faith and fell to their deaths. Sometimes bears crept up on them and attacked from behind. Their lives were lived on the edge, but somehow, inexplicably, they flourished.

The goats were expanding their range, moving south across the island in a slow wave, creating their homeland. From the front seat, the biologist pointed out the ones I had missed, traveling in single file up steep snowfields. We landed on a rocky platform, the helicopter leaving us to refuel in town. As the sound of the rotors receded, we crawled on our bellies to peer over at a small family group foraging below.

Wary of predators, the goats swiveled and stared up at us, their dark eyes unblinking. On the Olympic Peninsula in Washington State, the non-native goats were being removed, slung out in nets under helicopters. I wondered what it would be like to be removed so abruptly from a place, these later generations taken from the only home they had ever known, forced out to unknown ground. As I watched the goats, I knew there were people who faced the same fate every day and had done so all of the days in history. My wandering had been my choice, an indulgence instead of a necessity. At the same time, people had set off from known shores since the beginning of recorded history, putting their faith in small boats. Human migration was universal, a journey spurred by persecution, drought, or desire.

After a week, my husband returned, goatless and sunk into the same depression that shadowed him in town. Not speaking, as usual, he trudged into the garage to continue building guns. I listened for the sound of his footsteps on the stairs, knowing that a sense of unease had started to come with them.

I knew that as a wife, I should be his brace. The same way that I stabilized myself with a paddle on a stormy sea, I should be able to keep him afloat. But unlike my kayak, which responded immediately to the brace, he shrank from my efforts. It was too much, he said, he didn't want to talk. I buzzed ineffectually like a lost bee, aware I was pushing too hard, unable to stop.

Maybe it was our home that was the problem. I had bought it myself before we were married, and the dark carpet and walls reflected the overcast sky. The constant gloom required abundant lighting, and some days it felt as though the ceiling dropped lower and lower until we were submerged. Maybe a house that had more air and light would help us find the brightness we needed within ourselves.

I dragged him with me to look at a house we couldn't afford. "I love it," I argued, ignoring the hefty price tag. I didn't really love it, but it had promise. Much larger than our small home, it boasted floor-to-ceiling windows that looked out over the sea. Light flooded exuberantly into the open spaces. In a house like this, I thought, we could be happy. We would have space to spread out. Maybe if the house was large, our lives would not seem so small. We could have places to hide from each other, and the reasons we hid would not be so obvious. Our lowball offer was not accepted and I stopped looking. A new house would not solve this.

Sometimes, when I came back from walking the dog, I stood outside for a minute before going in. The cold rain dripped off my hat and down my face. The windows glowed bright and my heart ached. I wanted the atmosphere inside to be as warm as it looked, but I knew my husband's heart was closed to me. There were times when I thought he struggled to open the lock, but something always stopped him. There was such a chasm between us, and I could not figure out how to cross it. No amount of bracing was able to stop the inevitable capsize.

Wyatt had told me this, that the brace didn't always work. People got sloppy and let panic take over, slapping at the water at the wrong angle. All it took was one paddle slicing the water at the wrong angle, or mistaking the need for a high brace when you really needed a low.

I hadn't wanted to believe him. The kayaks were made for this type of ocean. They were stable crafts that would never let us down. If they could overturn so easily, in a second of human error, then what use was the brace? Why go out at all? Wyatt had no answers. You just had to practice the stroke, he had advised. Sure, you could hug the shore, where you could probably swim for it and survive if the cold water didn't get you first. What was the adventure in that, though? There was risk in everything. Practice the brace. Sooner or later, every paddler needed to use it.

two

In the wilderness, I moved through a world of men. Out on the coast, other women were few. Instead, I saw men: balancing on decks of salmon trollers, gliding in for the evening anchor; shaggy-haired bear hunting guides and their camo-clad clients, binoculars poised on deck as they slowly motored past the estuaries. Men walked big in this big world, spitting tobacco and spraying gunfire on remote beaches. Men staffed the weirs and the fish camps that dotted the isolated bays. Men piloted the midsize cruise ships that hovered in the strait, searching for whales. Even the rare kayakers we saw were men.

Swaddled in layers of wool and rubber, I began to feel androgynous, poised between the two extremes.

This was not unusual. For most of my life I had slipped through the boundaries of a world meant to keep women out. To survive I had become fluid, able to pass. I had learned to stay silent when the jokes and whiskey came out. I had learned to keep up when a man set a punishing pace to get to the top of a mountain, determined to drop me. In my last job, my boss told me they had been reluctant to hire a woman but had decided to take a chance. After all, he backpedaled, I would be working alone in remote country. What woman would want to do that? Unspoken was his thought: What woman could do that?

I was used to the language of men. They were loud and unfiltered. They said what they meant, even when their words scraped across a raw edge. I had fought fire with men, sleeping in still-warm ash on the mountainsides, carrying Pulaskis and shovels and chainsaw gas on forced marches through smoke that stung my eyes. I had cleared trails with men, pushing the crosscut saw back toward my partner as we chewed our way through a fallen giant. At times I had thought I could not be happier, sharing ham sandwiches and jokes with men in the wilderness.

But for paddling, I preferred women. The men I took along cursed the sea when it turned against us. They stumbled through camp before sunrise, oblivious to sleepers, intent upon coffee. We worked on their schedule: when they were hungry, we ate; when they were tired, we slept. They brought up reasons why we should not deviate from our chosen plan: too far, too difficult, too impossible. If we were stranded by weather, they paced the shoreline muttering about lost chances. They always wanted to take charge.

The women were not like that. They picked the easier line around the rocky cliffs, sought shelter in the kelp beds without apology. They stood in rubber boots on the bare black rocks finding delight in everything: the translucent shapes of fish in the shallows, alder-clad buildings peering out from the shore. When the sun came out, we cast off our fleece layers and let our hair fly like flags. We were no longer wives, daughters, mothers. We were released, free, wild. We were safe from dark alleys, unlit parking lots, the shadows of strangers following us, the constant low-level fear that dogged all women. This must be how men felt all the time, I thought.

Helga and I wove between the islands that dotted Necker Bay. We had paddled together so often that we moved in tandem, our strokes nearly matching. An unexpected sun glinted off the water drops flung from our paddle blades and made the ocean's surface sparkle with white light.

These islands were the first defense against the sea, and they looked it: beaches punished by winter storms, driftwood piled higher than we were tall far back into the forest. The sea never gave up here, constantly pushing forward and falling back in a ceaseless attack. The land itself was restless, whipped by hurricane-force winds and gouged by rain-driven land-slides. The whole place churned with an energy I could almost feel as we approached a possible take-out.

"Too much surf," I decided, studying the wave break onto the sandy beach. Helga nodded; as usual we were in sync with our decisions. There were no long discussions debating the merits of one route over another. We figured it out together, unlike the occasional man who accompanied me, who wanted to grab the maps and blaze the course.

I squinted into the sun, my sunglasses misplaced since I rarely needed them. We paddled around the island's flank to a protected cove. From there, we would walk across to the outer shore.

"What's on the other side?" Helga asked as we carried each boat to higher ground. We reached in the cockpits and pulled out the necessary gear: rifle, bullets, campsite monitoring sheets, camera, and trash bags.

"People camp over there," I said, lifting the rifle to my shoulder. I spilled a handful of extra slugs into my pocket. "Besides, did you see that sandy beach? There's supposed to be some kind of a driftwood hut too. Let's go check it out."

We hiked through a ragged line of forest, the line of the horizon visible on this narrow island. The interior was lumpy, as if someone had raked up the land into piles. The distinctive odor of skunk cabbage filled the air, and I pointed out where a bear had been digging out the plants. Bears ate it as a laxative after hibernating, and we were right on the edge between winter and spring.

My feet sank into deep sand. Somehow this beach existed in the middle of the wilderness, a half circle of gold ringed by evergreens. Sometime in the near past, a bear had wandered down this beach, its tracks a meander-ing line between tide line and forest.

But we were alone now. We trudged through the damp sand toward the far edge of the beach. A small hut stood there. The builders had carefully arranged driftwood silvered with age into a one-room cabin. Someone had painstakingly carved its name on the sill: The Elves' Hut. It did seem like a place for magic.

I prowled the cabin, looking for treasure and clues as to who had stayed here. A note was jammed between the driftwood planks, signed by two men and written to a woman: Audrey Sutherland. It talked about a route they were taking and said they were sorry to have missed her.

Audrey Sutherland! I felt an electric jolt of excitement. I had been following her trail for months. Though people spoke of her, sometimes I thought she wasn't real. We were just a few paddle strokes behind her, it seemed. If she really existed, she was a woman much older than I was, a woman who had been paddling this coast for years, always solo. Nobody knew when she would appear next, but she was seldom seen in towns, showing up only for resupply.

I had heard that in earlier years, she swam the coast of the Hawaiian island of Molokai in jeans, her possessions tied in a shower curtain, for the sheer sake of exploration. In Alaska she used a small inflatable kayak, hardly comparable to our high-tech boats. She built small campfires and gathered wild greens for her salads. She seemed to always pack out a bottle of wine. She seemed to never be afraid, not of big seas or of bears.

I stood at the Elves' Hut, staring out over the ocean, hoping to see the glint of a paddle. Audrey had just been here, or would be here soon. Where was she? Which bay did she traverse now? Was she even real? If we waited long enough, would she appear?

Of course, we couldn't wait. The nature of this job meant we moved on to a different camp nearly every night. There was no base camp where we could spread out and get comfortable. In order to keep doing these patrols, I had to show that they were worthwhile, and that meant constant motion. Sitting on the beach waiting for Audrey to show up would not cut it.

And I knew that this country was so big, someone could pass by and we would never know it. A whole flotilla could be pushing through the next arm of the bay, shielded from our sight by geography and weather.

It wouldn't be a comfortable stay in the hut. The roof was partially covered with what we liked to call the Alaska state flag—the ubiquitous, multipurpose blue tarp seen everywhere. In a heavy rain, water would collect on the tarp, bowing it until it shed a waterfall. Wind would whistle right through the arm-sized gaps in the wood. It was not a place built to last. A rough counter held pieces of translucent sea glass and someone had tried to fashion a cot of wood. It was more an idea of a shelter than a real one.

"I can't burn this one down," I told Helga. "No way," she agreed. Though it was our job to destroy human-made shelters in the wilderness, this whimsical hut seemed to fit here. Things were not always black and white. I vowed to keep this hut a secret. It wouldn't last through many more years of winter storms anyway.

A steady line of surf punished the beach. If it weren't for the temperatures, holding steady at the usual summer height of sixty, we could have been in the tropics.

We sat for a minute munching on snacks. I lay back, glumly contemplating the plastic bag of nuts and raisins. I had already picked out the M&M's on day one, and I was tired of what was left. I often overdosed on trail mix because it was easiest, contained in huge plastic bags, and I grabbed it by the handful from my deck bag. Most times we didn't have the right sea to stop for lunch, and trail mix was all we ate. When we could eat, we chose bagels, softened by the humidity. We would raft up together, our boats lifting and dropping with the slow swell. At night, no culinary wizardry took place; we usually dumped a packet of tuna into couscous or pasta and shredded some cheese over it. It didn't matter much. Gradually everything we ate took on the taste of the sea.

Reluctantly, we turned our backs on the Elves' Hut and returned to our boats. There were other islands to visit, garbage to collect, monitoring to be done. We had heard about an illegal trail that we suspected a guide had cut through the wilderness at the back of another bay, wielding a chainsaw and herding paying customers up to a lake in defiance of their permit. We needed to walk it and assess the damage, document the bridges built over the streams, stake it out in case someone appeared. There was always plenty to do.

As we stuffed our gear and ourselves back into our boats, I took one last scan of the island and the bay. I hoped to see a puffy inflatable narrowing the gap between me and the horizon, another woman making her way through the coastline.

But there was nobody else, just a black-winged sweep of rhinoceros auklets in the distance. Maybe tomorrow, I thought. There was always tomorrow. The currents washed up all sorts of things on the shore, things that made it to a certain beach only by chance. It wasn't so crazy that I could intersect paths with another woman out here who was writing her own story. She could tell me things; what it was like to swim along a forlorn coast, how and when to come back to shore.

three

"Look!" I hollered, pointing with my paddle. "People!"

Helga's eyes lit up with wonder. For weeks, we had seen only each other, wearing the same clothes, eating the same food, having the same conversations. We were bored with ourselves. Now we had spied some kayaks pulled up on a beach. In unison, we spun in their direction.

On rare, magical occasions like this, we saw other kayakers and steered our boats toward them, paddling in a frantic race to catch up. Sometimes we startled them, as though we were an invasion of two, chattering at full speed. Other times they found us, pulling into our camp to exchange greetings and look over maps.

This counted as a "wilderness encounter," another measure we were supposed to track. In other wildernesses I had worked in, it had not been uncommon to see two hundred people on a single trail at a time, groups of twos and threes bumping shoulders as they passed me on the narrow tread. In places like that, wilderness managers tried to adhere to what their planning documents said: no more than X encounters per day. This was supposed to ensure solitude, that ambiguous quality that meant something different to everyone. Invariably, there were more people than what the plan said there should be. Faced with tough choices, managers either established a quota or lottery for a trail system in the face of public opposition, or accepted the inevitable, that certain trails were going be more crowded than the optimistic planners had desired.

But here, in this wilderness, it was unusual enough to see others that we lingered at their camps, swapping sea stories way past when we should have been long gone. But most often we were alone, the only other people outlines in the distance. Sometimes they turned out to be mirages, a trick of light and water.

These kayakers were a father and son on a long trip down from Juneau. Bemused by the sight of two tousle-haired women paddling together, they lingered to pore over charts. We showed them where hidden freshwater seeped out of mossy rocks, and the good campsites we had discovered; we talked about the necessity of going into Lake Anna at slack. In return, they offered snacks and encouragement. We parted amicably, their boats heading south, ours north.

Alone again, we stroked over water hundreds of feet deep, yet so clear I could see farther down than I could measure. Dozens of moon jellyfish surrounded our boats. Shaped like parachutes, their bodies were so transparent that I could see the ocean through them.

Helga caught one on her paddle and held it up to the obscured sun, long tendrils hanging down like hair. Moon jellyfish, the most beautiful of jellies, bridal white, drifted with the current, unable to swim, and lived only about six months. Why were so many here, in this one place?

We speculated on this gathering. A nursery or some other reason had brought them in this large clump to the bay. Maybe they had come in with the tide and were waiting it out. As we passed through, a foamy wake of jellyfish parted behind us.

We beached at Mist Falls, a silvery cascade that roped its way down sheer cliffs. A fishery crew had built a trail of pure beauty, carving out railings of curved wood, constructing slim boardwalks and steps. Tourists could climb as far as the falls, where they would duck from the fine spray of water carried by wind to the overlook. The rest of us could go farther, on a rougher trail to the crew hut and an outhouse perched on a bench above. Since the crew held a permit to be there, with all the structures carefully plotted on the permit, we had to go check whether what they had built matched what they were supposed to have there.

The crew managed a flexible black pipeline and fish hatchery site, climbing up and down the trail dozens of times per day. They could swing up and down it with sacks of fertilizer and tools balanced carelessly on shoulders while I shimmied up more nervously. At the cabin, a shirtless man waved us inside. He showed no discomfort at our sudden arrival, as if two women showing up was a normal thing. He didn't put on his shirt.

This was a place where anything could happen, two ocean-rough women showing up out of the blue. He served us tea and stilted conversation, as though he had forgotten how to talk. Helga and I eyed each other. We were becoming like that on the sea sometimes.

We walked as far as we could go, to where the outhouse stood. It perched overlooking the long reach of Chatham Strait and, in the distance, Admiralty Island, its peaks wreathed in snow. "This is the best view of any outhouse I've ever seen," I said, and Helga agreed.

I had always thought that geography had its hand in shaping personality, and the isolation of the outer coasts seemed to say that this was true. In Florida, I had known unhurried, gentle people, sweet as the sugar sand under our feet. In the desert, locals were spare and direct, sometimes unyielding. Here, the people we met in our travels seesawed between two extremes. Coming in for a landing, we braced ourselves. We never really knew what we would get.

At a lonely fish weir, we found only an empty shack, the workers we had seen onshore vanishing completely. They had run into the woods, we realized, and were lurking there somewhere, squatting on their heels, waiting for us to leave. Hostility hung over the rough dwelling like smoke. I could feel eyes upon us as we documented the condition of the hut and trail, under permit to the Forest Service.

"Gone bush," the old-timers called this, and I could understand. With only Helga and the waves to talk to, I had developed a wilderness shorthand that only we could understand. Living out here for months, the weir tenders must have been dismayed or frightened by our brash intrusion.

At Little Port Walter, the people onshore waved enthusiastically. They gabbed at us in speeds that were hard to decipher. It was difficult to pry ourselves away, and it was obvious they wanted us to stay long past when the tide would let us.

In Port Alexander, at the very bottom of Baranof Island, our arrival was preceded by tides of suspicion. Later we heard that uneasy residents had rowed their marijuana plants across to the less accessible side of town, worried we might confiscate them. Law was nonexistent in that place, and none of us really cared what people grew in such a small outpost.

On a walk later, I spied several plants, thick trunked as small trees. The people who owned them made themselves scarce. Everyone had their addiction of choice out here. "The people who live here," one resident explained, "they really can only live here. Know what I mean?"

≈

With the birth of her child, Helga was temporarily lost to me, immersed in a world of diapers and play dates. We spoke different languages now. She could go on only occasional patrols. Her heart was elsewhere.

"You can't go alone," Sven had warned. I had imagined it that way, paddling solo through the misty islands that choked the Chichagof coast. I chafed with the demands of a partner, one who was not Helga. Often it was hard. One man arose in the predawn, setting up unbreakable rules: nobody was to talk to him in the first two hours of the day, and we had to steer clear of certain subjects that caused him to explode in anger. Others slept in, disregarding the best paddling time before the winds began to blow. I had to watch out for them, making sure they brought the right stuff, knew how to avoid the rocks, and didn't run from bears. It was far better, I thought, to go it alone.

But Sven laid down the law, and after miles of paddling, each partner taught me something I had forgotten. They marveled at the way purple sea stars clustered on the black rocks before the tides swept in to draw them back out to sea. They saw the little things I had begun to overlook: the bullet-shaped bodies of fish in a hundred feet of water, slipping under our boats. The shiver of pressing our hands and feet into the depressions the bears left as they traveled through the spongy ground under the spruce trees.

For a time, I had a series of temporary kayak partners, unschooled in the ocean beyond their small town. They usually lasted only one trip, the wind and rain doing a number on their desire. After a few days, all of them were ready to go home. If the plane was late, if Captain Johnny couldn't bash through the swell to get us on time, they eyed the satellite phone with longing. They mentioned events they could not possibly miss. They pointed with optimism at temporary blue spotting the sky.

They held up canisters of bear spray and asked how it worked. They trusted me to find the way back to our boats from the alpine lakes far above. We hunkered on our heels watching bears pass by our tents, and they watched me for a sign that things were about to go south, or not. They wanted to know everything: why we burned outlaw cabins, why the out-fitters were allowed to stalk bears in the estuaries, why I didn't want to go home, even when the gales kept us trapped onshore and no plane or boat could retrieve us for days.

By now I had learned to read the charts I carried, stowed in a water-proof case and strapped to the kayak deck. In the office, I walked to the map case and unfurled the chart I needed, taking note of what was shown and what was not. My new partners and I knelt over the charts in camp as I pointed out our route.

It took hours sometimes to navigate past one point; it was easier to stow the maps and hope for the best. Instead, as we paddled, I passed on the stories I had learned.

Though I would never be a local, I was the teacher now. I pointed out landmarks: This beach, curved like a smile, had no name, but it let you know you were nearly out to the White Sisters. That was where you made the decision: stay or go. This small bight was where Helga and I had nearly lost our tents to the tide. I passed on the old stories too, not knowing what was truth and what was fiction.

The only thing I did know, the story I made up about myself, was that I knew how to navigate the ocean.

I paddled out as far as I dared, miles out, so far that the town was a dim outline. I threaded my way through the outside islands. Out there, I saw the long, slow, rolling backs of waves born far from where I dipped my paddle into liquid. In the kayak, on the ocean, I was more graceful than I could ever be on land.

People noticed. "You're so brave," they said. I let them think it, but it wasn't really true. When the big swells rolled in, ten feet, twelve feet, I clutched my paddle in hands gone white. I sang, loudly and off-key, to drown out the hiss of waves coming up behind me. I braced, slapping my paddle down hard onto sea that felt like concrete, in order to stay upright. None of this was easy.

But it was far easier than facing my disintegrating marriage, a place I was finding harder to navigate through. There were no charts that showed the hidden rocks, no coast pilot guide to tell me where the safe anchorages were. This was unknown territory.

When it was finally winter and the bay was free from the summer craziness of dodging cruise ships, I tried to paddle out one last time before putting my boat away for the season. Pools of freshwater had moved out from the streams and formed a freezing layer on top of salt that I had never seen before. I banged on the plates of ice with my paddle, trying to force a way through, but there was none. Sitting trapped in ice that closed behind me, cutting off my escape route, I realized that sometimes there was no way through.

You could kayak in winter, but it was hard. You had to get out there in the brief window between dawn and early twilight. You had to bundle up in all the clothes you could possibly imagine. Nobody else was out there but you. There was no hope for rescue.

The stakes were higher, and as the winter came down the mountain, snow level falling farther every day, you had to admit it was time to stop. That it was too dangerous to continue. The story of the tourists who fell out of their boats near No Thorofare Bay while battling a rising tide, their bodies stacked frozen on the dock, weighed heavily on my mind each time I tried to go out. This might have been true or it might have been a fable. It didn't matter. I was brave, but not brave enough.

|

wet exit

You probably don't want to leave your boat, but sometimes you must. Slithering out of the cockpit can be done either with grace or in a flustered panic. Say you find yourself upside down, and you haven't learned the roll. You are trapped underwater. There is no other choice: you are going to have to exit.

The hardest part is releasing the spray skirt. This semicircle of nylon seems impossible to escape when you are fighting to breathe. This is the time to be patient. Run your hands along its edge and find the loop where you have stretched it tight along the top of the cockpit. Hopefully you haven't made a mistake and tucked it underneath. If all is well, you should be able to grab the loop and pull it free. Now kick yourself out from under the boat and gulp a big breath of air.

It will feel like you're underwater forever, but it is likely less than a minute. You can stand anything for a minute to gain your freedom.

one

"Don't make your man your woman," Helga advised. We strolled along a trail close to town, harvesting salmonberries. The soft fruit fell apart in my fingers; you had to be gentle with each one. They packed a punch in the mouth; you never knew whether the first bite would be sweet or tart. You took your chances with salmonberries.

We ate them anyway. How could we resist? When I picked a good one, it was a burst of flavor that was like stored sunshine. There were so many we could not pick them all; we shared them with the bears. There could be a bear in these bushes right now, I realized, and shrugged. I had come a long way from the scared woman who had carried bear spray everywhere. I was still afraid when it mattered, but you couldn't carry a constant cloak of fear with you all the time. It got too heavy.

Don't make your man your woman.

I knew she was right. One person could not fill all the empty spaces the way the high tide covered a beach. Women were for late-night confidences over a campfire, secrets that you kept inside seeping out, words you could never say to any man. But what I meant wasn't those things.

It was hard to explain. Some women loved the idea of the Alaskan man who chopped a cord of firewood with an ax, flew a plane, and never, ever showed a single emotion. But living with stone took its toll. Even the land relented to the sea; nothing was impervious. I had seen it myself. Keeping others out had left me as lonely as waking up under another gray sky felt, day after day without sun to warm my bones.

I felt foolish, trying to describe what was missing. I knew what my inner voice would say. *Needy. Emotional.* My husband had echoed those thoughts. Something was wrong with me, he said. Not him. I had kept biting at him the way the ocean nibbled off chunks of land, until the land finally gave in. He crossed his arms. He wasn't going to change, he said again. I had to be the one to do it. After a time, I had learned what the ocean already knew: you recognized the cliffs you could not breach. I stopped trying. We drifted apart even more, solitary islands separated by different passages.

≈

I was thinking about exits, trying the idea out loud. I remembered how Wyatt's class had floated around in Silver Bay practicing wet exits. The hardest thing to commit to was the actual exit, the sudden immersion in water so cold that it could, theoretically, stop a heart. Even in a dry suit, the water pooled under my collar and lurked, an ominous presence, slowly dripping down my back. My veins clogged with ice as I fumbled with a slippery, obstinate boat. It was no comfort to know that most people, if they survived the initial trauma of falling in the water, could survive about thirty minutes. I heard an invisible clock ticking in my head as I struggled to complete the steps Wyatt had laid out for us in the warm comfort of the classroom.

Still, once you committed to it, it was never as bad as you feared. In fact, I sometimes laughed as the boat tipped and I slid inexorably toward the cold, waiting arms of the ocean. Sometimes the thinking about it was worse than the reality. It had been a relief to finally be in the water, working through the steps that meant a rescue.

I knew I had been trying too hard. I had pursued my husband relentlessly, trying to unlock his heart. I wanted to know what he was thinking in the hours he stayed silent. I wanted him to turn inside out, unleash the dreams, doubts, and fears he carried. I wanted to see the entire person, not just the slice he allowed me to see, the one that was clamped down in the grip of an invisible vise. Like the winter-shy bears who heard us coming on the trails, he had fled in the other direction.

We went to marriage counseling, in a building where there were other offices peopled by strangers and friends. I crept up the stairs, feeling as if everyone in town must know that we were driven to this last-ditch effort. In the stuffy room, I clutched at tissues; my husband glared. It was hard to sum up everything that was wrong in a few sentences. "Your husband won't talk to you?" I stuttered to a stop, feeling foolish.

"She doesn't love you anymore," the counselor said bluntly, and I cringed. Was that really true? That seemed so black and white. So final. There were moments I believed that I could choose to retreat to the woman I had been, first married in a sparkly dress. But the love had been dissolved over time, water eroding a rock wall, and I could find only pieces of it, not enough to fashion anything into a whole cloth.

The counselor sighed. I imagined that she thought we were beyond hope. She turned to my husband. "Here's an assignment. Come home from work, sit on the couch next to your wife, and tell her something about your day. Not what you did, but what you felt about one aspect of your day. Try it for half an hour every day."

Next to me, my husband stiffened, but he agreed to try it. We trooped out of the office, leaving in separate cars.

The next afternoon, I perched on the couch as my husband's footsteps stomped onto the porch. He came in, shedding his coat onto the floor. He sat. I watched him hopefully. Just one crumb, I thought. One word would be enough.

He said nothing. He shook his head. After a few minutes he got up and shuffled downstairs to work on his gun project.

A sudden rage swept over me, the first bloom of anger I had let myself feel. There had been enough anger in our house already; it hung like unseen smoke in the rooms. You could feel it as soon as you walked in, which is why I suspected many of our friends had faded away, or saw me on neutral ground: the running trails, the ocean. I had my own friends now, friends my husband didn't know. I trailed him downstairs, wanting an explanation.

"It's just outside my comfort zone," he said, not looking at me. It was cold in the garage and I shivered, tears in my eyes.

"Talking to me is outside of your comfort zone?"

Yes, it was, he explained. He was just wired this way, he repeated. I imagined a team of tiny workers in his brain, connecting red and blue wires, the zap of a missed connection.

There was nothing left to say. I turned and went upstairs, where it should have been warm. Instead, a chill I could not shake penetrated deep into my bones. I could see no way out.

But I had learned from kayaking that there was always a way. Even in the tightest of constricted passages, there was always a sliver that allowed us to worm our boats through. Even the bays that drained dry at low tide filled up again. In a motorboat, there had been times that Sven and I had given up, called it a day. That bight was too shallow, always, even at high tide, for us to venture in. That route between two islands was studded with rocks that would break our motor. In yet another spot, kelp lay in thick mats, enough to foul our prop. We made do with what we could accomplish, throwing up our hands in defeat. It was good enough.

With kayaks, though, anything seemed possible. Storms blew themselves out eventually, allowing me to cross the unprotected coast. If I carried my boat onto a rocky shore, I wouldn't puncture its soft skin on the teeth of rocks. Bears couldn't get our food if we hung it in the trees or protected it in bear canisters. I always knew there was a way, even though it was never easy. There were casualties sometimes, bumps and scrapes to the fiberglass, wet-skin blisters on hands. In life, it seemed, just as in kayaking, you had to decide what you could live with and what you could overcome. Then you were left with the consequences. It was time to decide.

"It's time for our long run," Peter said on the phone. I looked out the window with trepidation. A steady downpour pounded the street. The temperature hovered at forty, a sure recipe for hypothermia.

Still, I had said I would run long, so I sighed and geared up: Lycra tights, ball cap, long-sleeved synthetic shirt, light rain jacket. I would be soaked within seconds.

"We'll just try for twelve and see how we do," Peter offered, sensing my reluctance to venture out into the storm. I knew we would end up running more than twelve miles. We always did.

Outside Whale Park, we took our first running steps and both groaned. The first four miles, we had determined, were the hardest. After that, our bodies resigned themselves to the next miles and it became easier.

I had been training for a marathon that winter. Winter running was what I did when I couldn't paddle, and this season had been worse than most, both on the ocean and on land. The rain bulleted out of the sky with a ferocity that limited my enthusiasm. Both sky and water matched; a sullen gray with no separation. The sun had not come out since October.

There was no hope for going out in kayaks in such stormy seas; though I had often paddled in small craft advisories, this was beyond what would be safe. Even the channels in front of town were whipped to an angry froth. The forecasts called for gales, waves up to thirty feet. The surfers gathered on the far side of Kruzof, exulting in the swell. My kayak collected layers of old leaves as it lay near the house, unused.

I ran twelve, sixteen, twenty-two miles, without music, just the slap of my shoes on wet pavement. Peter and I dared the fish hatchery road in late fall, dodging salmon carcasses just dropped by bears, singing at the top of our lungs to warn them we were coming. There were only fourteen miles of road in town if you didn't count the side streets and the route to the airport, so we doubled back, taking in familiar ground. Once we reached the campground at the end of the road, we turned around and went back the way we had come until we had run far enough.

During those runs, we sometimes talked, when we had the breath. Peter had retired recently and moved onto a sailboat. He had met someone, a woman who wasn't from Alaska, but who he hoped would stay. You sometimes had to import, hoping the person would fall in love with the place like you had. Peter was betting on difficult odds, but he remained optimistic.

I told Peter I was thinking about leaving, both my husband and the island, but that there were times I couldn't imagine it. Then again, there were times I could. I gestured at the scene around us: dense evergreens guarded the road, armor against the tide. In the distance, the ocean seethed with the storm. What I saw was both magnetic and frightening, but undeniably alive. "How could I leave this?" I asked, knowing there was no right answer.

Peter ran along checking his GPS watch and commenting on our pace. Nine minutes per mile, eight-thirty, ten on that last hill. We should aim for nine, he decided, a long run pace we could maintain. We both wanted to break four hours, so we would have to put some time in the bank during the actual race, he said. He did not say one way or the other which direction I should take other than that. He often sprinted ahead to beat the clock and then fell back from the effort. I tried to keep a steady pace instead, a pace that would get me through the miles.

You could quit in a marathon, and I thought about it as I ran my first race on a spring day in Napa Valley, the weather a good fifty degrees above what we had trained in. Peter surged near me at mile sixteen. "I've hit the wall," he panted and fell back. I had lost my other friends near the five-mile mark. I was surrounded by strangers, all of us intent on an arbitrary finish line, all of us there for our own reasons.

At mile twenty the course steepened with a long incline. The runners around me slowed. Some of them started to walk, giving up. What was the point? None of us were going to win, anyway.

It would be easy to quit here, I thought. Slip into the crush of people who watched the race, drop out at an aid station. Who would know? Who would care?

I would. *One more mile*, I told myself. One more mile for all the others Peter and I had run together on days when it felt like nobody else was out there but us. For the ocean miles too, the unknown distances between where we were and a safe landing.

At three-quarters of a mile to go, a speedier friend who had finished half an hour before appeared by my side. "Almost done!" he said. The distance seemed impossible. Six minutes, seven? I had gone beyond anything resembling pain miles before, but the effort to put one foot in front of the other seemed too great.

Unable to respond, I ignored him. This fight was mine alone. My pace slowed further. I thought it over: I could just walk it in, like the others I saw in front of me. There was no shame in walking. Or I could summon up one last bit of grit and finish.

For a moment, I was back in the junior high pool, clutching at the slippery wall, frozen in place. I was on a bike, its wheels sliding around underneath me. I was different from everyone.

I thought also of the ocean and the times when the tide and wind had been stacked against me, my boat's bow buried under the mouths of waves, the hiss of surf at my back. There hadn't been a choice then.

You're wrong, I said to the voice that had defined me most of my life. *Wrong about not being able to finish this race, wrong about not being brave.* I would not give up, not this time. I spurred myself to the semblance of a jog and crossed the finish line.

My husband had stayed home, so only my running friends congratulated me at the finish line. We gathered in a sweaty group hug, all of us having overcome our own thoughts of quitting. Most of our times weren't great, a shade over the four hours we had hoped to break, but they were still good enough for us, at least this time. There was always hope for the next time, when we would surely do better.

"When's the next one?" Peter said. "Let's do another!"

As I stood there, it came to me that I had been telling myself other fictions all these years. Though I had done outwardly hard, brave things like fighting fire, in other ways I had chosen easy exits, choosing to believe that my balance was poor, a certain recipe for failing at riding a bike. I had told myself that I didn't really want to swim, instead of the actual truth, that I was afraid of trying and failing as I had done before. I had chosen to believe that I was unlovable, that I was too different, a stranger in the world.

As I clutched my medal, I realized something else. No matter how many miles I ran, no matter how high the seas in which I paddled, I would always feel different from everyone else. There was no getting away from it. But for the first time, I thought it might be possible not to care.

three

By now, five years in, when the rains came in for good, I was prepared. I set up a bright light panel by my desk to simulate the sun. When I left the office for my midday run, I had once wrapped myself in layers of rain gear, but now I ran in only a T-shirt and shorts, returning soaked to wipe down with paper towels in the bathroom. It was only rain, a constant backdrop. I knew how to handle it.

My friends from down in the states called. "You're still up there?" they asked. "When are you leaving?"

"I'm staying," I said, believing it.

"Forever?" They didn't believe it. They sent me job announcements in exotic places—Hawaii, Arizona. How could I pass up the chance to move back up the ladder? I didn't want to become what was commonly termed a dinosaur: a worker who augered in, unable to adapt to new ways of thinking.

But there was something appealing about knowing a place, even if it put me in that category. "He's been here forever," people said about Sven. But they also went to him with questions. The best place to anchor in Black Bay, the history of the abandoned Boomer property with its silent bulldozers and leaking oil drums. It seemed good to know these things.

As settled as I told myself I was, I knew that I was seeing only a small sliver of Alaska. The rest of it lurked, big and wild, outside the boundary of the archipelago. If I were to call this state home, I wanted to know more of it.

≈

In Alaska's interior, I fell into step with a man from a native village, his hair twisted into a long graying braid down his back. "You're from Sitka?" he asked. "That's just a suburb of Seattle to us." He laughed. "This is the real Alaska."

Billy and I were both here on the banks of the Kuskokwim River patrolling a fire started by blueberry pickers seeking warmth. I had volunteered to come up here to fight fire in a year that the rains had held off, trading the ocean for the land. Because I still had fire qualifications, Sven had allowed me to go, even though that meant nobody would be out patrolling in kayaks. In this dry year, fire was burning up the black spruce heart of the state, and everyone was needed.

To get to this fire, I had flown over hundreds of miles of tundra, the pilot calmly rustling a newspaper as he flew. The land itself had unfurled beneath us as though it were an ocean itself, unbroken by villages or people. Huge fires chewed up the landscape, unattended. Our plane was so small and the country so big. How did people ever find home here?

The urgency of the first hours had faded and we talked strategy as we circled the fire, still glowing hot on the edges. In the distance a portable pump droned, delivering river water to the burning tundra. Two crews hustled along the line, training hoses on hot spots. Dusk, or as close as it got here in the middle of summer, would fall soon. Musk oxen had been spotted to the south, and I peered out over the flat blankness, hoping to spot one.

We finished rehashing the next day's plan: a hoselay stretching from the portable pumps to encircle the fire, a complete mop-up of the interior until no smokes remained. I studied Billy as we walked, our boots sinking deep in the ashes. As often happened on the fireline, we shared stories of our lives, the things that mattered to us. He told me his: trips to his fish camp, on a different river, one his ancestors had built. His native Dena'ina language, still spoken. The time he had been trapped by fire and lifted out just in time via helicopter. He laughed about that one—after all, he had survived. He didn't need maps the way I did: he had the interior memorized by the fires he had fought in each place. He had been a teenager when he had started fighting fire; his father had been a firefighter before him. He would hang on as long as he could, he said.

Listening to him, I was hearing another definition of home. His was an unbroken chain of ancestors, a belonging to a place that was unquestioned. It never occurred to him to even think about living anywhere else. This was what you did—you were born, lived, and died on one piece of ground.

≈

I knew I could never adopt a place and feel the same way he did. The great-granddaughter of immigrants, and a woman who had hopscotched over land that had been forcibly taken from others, I had a tenuous connection at best. Staring out over the vast expanse of river delta, I realized that my search for belonging seemed frivolous to people like Billy. Even to travel the country looking for it showed how much privilege I carried with me. It was true too that here in the interior, there hadn't been a word like "wilderness," a separation between humans and the land. I had always looked at the land as if it should bend to accommodate me as I decided whether I loved it enough to stay. I had discarded places and men for reasons that no longer seemed necessary: the country had been too plain, too stark, too tropically hot; the men too simple, too fat, too old. I had been looking at my journey as if I was owed something by love and place, when in fact it was the opposite.

Billy didn't need to spend time contemplating his place in the world. Instead, he was chuckling over what had happened in McGrath: I had been reading a book he loaned to me, waiting for the next callout, and a firefighter had cranked up a nearby beater truck. Oil flew from every orifice of the truck, landing on the book's pages. Apologetically I had given the book back, now ruined. "Don't sit so close to that truck next time," Billy said, his dark eyes shining. It was clear that his life held equal parts sorrow and joy, but he chose to weigh the joy higher.

When we got back to camp, his crew eyed me politely. They would lean on their tools and listen to what I said about corralling the fire, but all of us knew that they would always know more than I did. They carefully set up their shelters far from where I had pitched my tent. At night, I could hear their laughter through the trees, but I wasn't invited over. I didn't blame them. I was an outsider here. I would go home. They were already there.

Their version of home was one I would never know. I wasn't native to a landscape the way they were, generations before them fanning out over the deltas and the rivers, calling them by their real, first names. I was aware of how much I didn't know about the first inhabitants, things I would never expect to know. Theirs was a story ten thousand years old and rooted in place, a homeland that was taken from them, my white skin forever a reminder.

I went back to my tent and lay inside, listening to the silence of the interior. Occasionally a tree exploded in flame, lighting the inside of my tent like the moon. Unknown birds flapped through the semidarkness. This was as far from the ocean as I could get, but the country here reminded me of it, the implacable way it stretched out for miles, unbroken by anything except low shrubs.

I wouldn't have a home like they did, but I could learn from them. They used the tools they had to make a temporary home at our fire camp: shelters strung with rope and black plastic, a set of hooks where they could hang their tools. They insisted on hauling a coffeepot along with them as they walked the line, stringing up a tarp and making a brew. In this desolate place, they were more at home than most people were in their own houses.

They watched the fire gobble up the black spruce with impassive looks on their faces. They remembered the last time this country had burned, and the time before that. Their fathers and mothers remembered the fires before that. The same ground would burn again and their children would remember. I wondered what it would be like, that certainty as you woke up that you would always be here. How it would be not to feel the invisible clock ticking inside your bones, telling you to go, always to go.

Although we had a full shift the next day, I could not sleep. I lay staring up at the nylon that separated me from the night sky. I knew I had turned a corner in an invisible road and there was no going back. I knew with a cold certainty that I would never find home in the life I was leading. I was thinking about the exit, and it no longer seemed like something to fear. I could imagine the immersion, the shock of the cold water. I could picture the moment when I was able to right my floating boat, climb aboard, bail out what I no longer needed, and paddle away. People did that. They took whatever talismans they needed to make a home wherever they were.

self-rescue

You need to know how to rescue yourself, from the sea or from life. Hopefully you have not forgotten the tools to make it possible: a bilge pump and a paddle float. Hopefully you have hung on to your boat and your paddle. Hopefully, you can find balance. In a self-rescue, stability is your friend.

There are several ways to self-rescue, some easier than others. But don't fool yourself. Sometimes, despite your best efforts, a self-rescue does not work. The deck may just be stacked against you.

one

The self-rescue was not hard when the ocean was flat. Once you had tipped and slid easy as butter out of your boat, you maneuvered around to the stern and flipped it back over—no simple feat if it was waterlogged, but possible in light winds. Then you took your paddle float and attached it to the end of the paddle, using it as a stabilizer to slither back into the cockpit.

Here was where you had to pay attention. The boat would be a floating barge, sloshing with half the ocean, it seemed. Any sudden moves and it would list to one side, tipping you out again. Each step had to be carefully executed, despite your fingers turning white with cold and your rising panic. You had to reach for your bilge pump and slowly, painstakingly force water out over the side. This could take several minutes. The whole time you had to keep an eye on your paddle, wedge it between your knees so it didn't break free and end up washed away by the current. When the boat was bailed out, you could begin to paddle again. By that time, you would probably be nearly hypothermic, and finding landfall would be the most pressing step.

Wyatt drilled it into us: keep hold of your boat. Losing a paddle would be a calamity, but that was why we strapped an extra one to our back deck. Losing the boat meant losing all but the thinnest margin of survival. Hold on as long as you can to that boat, he told us. We had all heard the stories of people who had not. One year a crew of forest workers took a flat-bottomed boat to check a fish weir at the edge of a lake. At the place where the water cascaded from the lake into the ocean, they tipped, no life vests on board. The boat broke free and plummeted over the falls. Two swam to shore. The last person was never found. There were other stories, all of which hit the point home: stick with your boat as long as you can.

In case of catastrophe, separation from my boat, I carried enough supplies in my life vest to last a few hours, should I be lucky enough to claw my way to land. A couple of Clif Bars; emergency flares; waterproof matches; a small VHF radio, the telephone of the sea, in the front chest pocket; and the EPIRB I always kept strapped to my body. This was a small black cartridge with a handle to pull if I got in trouble. Theoretically, my coordinates would be sent to the nearest search-and-rescue unit. Theoretically, help would soon be on the way.

Realistically, I knew that this was only a fine line between life and death. Starting a fire in the rain was one of the hardest things to do, and a lot of people did it wrong. They panicked, setting entire trees ablaze, or never succeeded, running through all their firestarter in their impatience and fear. You had to be patient in the rain.

The old-timers showed me how. We hiked deep into the old forest, gathering wisps of lichen as fragile as baby hair. We reached under fallen logs to scoop up sheltered pieces of bark and twigs. We scraped amber resin with our thumbnails in the places where trees had been wounded. We built the fires on the beach, where the high tide would wash away the traces. We leaned over the embers, shielding them from the weather, willing them to blaze. If you followed the old-timers' advice, it always worked.

But in the end, self-rescue was hard. In the water I became a cumbersome being, my paddle float slipping off, the paddle itself an unwieldy thing. Practicing, I floundered in the swimming pool, losing my nerve.

Other boats clogged the lap lanes, the chance of collision with capsized students high.

Meanwhile, Wyatt showed off, demonstrating the cowboy method of self-rescue. In one graceful movement, he leaped upon the stern of his boat, straddling it and using his feet and hands to drop into the cockpit. He bowed to our applause. All of us knew we hadn't a prayer of attempting that approach.

During one effort, I looked up while clutching the side of my kayak and caught the eye of a hunting guide, walking past the foggy windows. He smirked and waved. This probably looked crazy to him. What did we know of the sea? People like me came and went, leaving no impression. Already several of my coworkers had bailed for the easier life down south, places with lawns to water, roads to drive.

I knew how to rescue myself. I had done it all my life. I had learned early on that nobody would save me but myself. Traveling alone across the country meant you had to know how to fix a flat, drive on black ice, put on your own chains. As a wilderness ranger, I had to get myself across rivers that boiled up to my waist, scramble up over trailless mountain passes, and carry my own backpack, which towered over my head, topping out at over seventy pounds. Rescue was easy when you had nobody you could depend on. There was no other choice.

"Keep trying," Wyatt said, even though some students had given up and headed for the showers. I tipped over one more time. Feet floppy in the deep end, I attached the paddle float to the blade. With a desperate lunge, I slithered into the boat like a seal.

"Perfect," he said. "Try it again."

Though this was far from the sea, where there would be more to worry about than onlookers or collisions, nailing the self-rescue unstuck a part of me that had never believed in myself.

Around me the water churned as the remaining students flipped and rescued themselves amid laughter. I sat up tall in my unstable boat, preparing for another self-rescue.

The inner voice piped up in one last effort. It had been getting softer these past few years, sometimes nearly a whisper, sometimes gone entirely. *You're going to mess up. You'll never be good at this. And by the way, you look terrible in that bathing suit.*

I took a deep breath of the humid, chlorine-soaked air. It was time for the voice to fade. There were times it had served me well; trying to mute it, I had pushed myself to walk the edge of what I thought possible. But in the end, it had stuck, refusing to believe in me. I wasn't sure how, but I knew that in order to rescue myself, I had to stop listening.

And then another thought came to me. I had spent so many years trying to fit in. I had tried to cover up what I believed was different about me by taking on brave things: moving across the country alone, fighting fire. Keeping myself unknown to others. It was what I had first thought after the marathon: maybe I didn't need to fit in. Maybe I could be someone like Audrey Sutherland, a woman some would call eccentric, a woman who was free.

I closed my eyes, flipped my boat, and believed.

two

I had been in Alaska for two years when my kayak instructor decided the only way out was the gun.

Sometimes our island felt like both a prison and a refuge. The rest of the world seemed distant, as if in another galaxy, circling a different sun than ours. Other places I had lived, I had felt closer to the rest of the world. There, you could drive away, and in a few hours or days, you could leave desert for mountains, snow for ocean. The highways ran like arteries across the Lower 48, connecting my little town to bigger ones. The news of gunmen in schools or women disappearing off the streets made it seem like it could happen anywhere there. But here, what was more immediate lay right outside our doors: the threat of a tsunami, a landslide, a bear strolling through a neighborhood. It was hard to care, sometimes, about the less immediate outer world.

I felt as though I lived in a bubble, a curtain of rain and the width of the sea separating us from everyone else. I even now called going to the Lower 48 states "going to America," the way everyone else did, as though we were our own country. I was both insulated and isolated all at once.

Wyatt and I talked only about the ocean and the boats we paddled across it. We hunkered in his tiny shop, discussing the merits of a Necky over a Current Designs. We debated stability; the trade-off required between a fast, zippy boat versus one that handled like a wide, slow tank. Plastic boats that you could drag heedlessly over beach cobble or swifter fiberglass ones that you had to baby every time you came to shore. He winced when I brought a boat in to be repaired, the fiberglass shell deeply bruised. You had to be careful with glass boats, he warned me, because for something so strong, they were fragile underneath. It didn't take much to wound them beyond repair.

He could fix it, he said, but it would never really be the same.

We studied the mechanics of the roll, a way to save yourself if you capsized. Sometimes, he said, you didn't want to exit the boat. In big surf, the kayak could get away from you, and that meant certain disaster. You had to have more tools in your arsenal. In the pool, he demonstrated the roll, dipping into the water in one controlled motion and popping back up with a grin.

There were other dangers too. The man who had owned the kayak shop before Wyatt did had died doing a roll, his head banging into a rock below the ocean's surface. I thought of that every time I went under, wondering what was unseen, what waited below to kill me.

I tried over and over again but could not complete it, ending up clinging to the side of a swamped boat. Sometimes a brace can't save you, Wyatt told me. Keep trying, you'll get it. I never did, though. He believed I could, and that was enough.

My boat was too big for my small frame, he said, trying to make me feel better. It was true: I swam inside the cockpit. To pull off a good roll, you had to fit inside like a hand in a glove. That meant the uncertainty of a slimmer boat, though, and I sought stability over the roll.

To die by your own hand in June is to mean it. I often thought that November was the month that would push people over the edge. November was when an invisible spigot turned on in the sky and never quit. Gales whipped up the ocean to a merciless froth. You stayed close to home in November. You had to.

We stopped going out on kayak patrol. It would be unsafe now, with the coast deserted of travelers. There would be entire weeks when we would be unreachable by plane or boat because of lowering sky and high seas.

This was the time of year none of us liked. Spring seemed far away and the light grew less every day until we had barely five hours to spare from the darkness. We spent November cleaning up all the gear, hanging the dry suits, winterizing the water filters, scrubbing down the boats and storing them behind the maintenance garage. This was when we hunched over our computers, writing up reports of all the campsites we had inventoried, the cabins we had burned. We sat in meetings, our wild souls temporarily tamed. The lucky ones who could afford it escaped to Hawaii, returning with a quickly disappearing tan. It was a time of year when hope was likely to wink out in those who were fading already. I never felt that kind of despair, but I did sit as close as I could to my light panel, substituting it for sun. I sprinted outside whenever the sun did shine, turning my face up like a flower. On really bad days, there were clumps of us outdoors, shifting our positions each time a cloud broke to reveal light. Along with many others, I counted the days until spring.

But this was June, the best month of all. It was possible to believe that this summer might be the exception, that the sun would fight off the clouds all season long. The days stretched precious and endless, beginning at three in the morning and conceding only around midnight. We all became a little manic in June, trying to fit it all in. Children ran feral at midnight and we started hikes up Harbor Mountain in late evening. We could sleep in November.

The news ran like a virus through our town. As soon as I could get away, I slipped into my kayak and shoved off with no clear destination. As I paddled with sure, clean strokes, I thought of the paddler's box, the technique Wyatt had taught me in class so long ago. This was a beginner's concept but one that took years to grasp. In a small boat on a big ocean, a new kayaker wanted to become bigger than she was. You wanted to lean over the boat with big strokes, as if this would make you go faster or farther. Some people never learned that to paddle was to submit to the sea. I saw them off the cruise ships, paddles striking the air with force, way higher than they needed to be. These people never made it very far. Instead, you wanted a stroke that could sustain you, push you farther than you thought possible.

Wyatt's shop was a cramped space but it had been full of possibility. Kayaks of all shapes hung from the walls. There were paddles ranging from the wildly expensive featherlight to the more prosaic plastic models. One day when I complained about how hard it was to lift my heavy boat over my head and onto the saddles of the rack, he pounced on a box and brought it to me. "Hully Rollers," he said. The little rolling wheels allowed me to position the bow of my boat at the back edge of the truck and lunge forward, catapulting the kayak into place. It was a life and back saver.

Could any of us have saved his life? I thought of all the banal conversations we had shared over the past several years. Why had we spent so much time discussing the scull, a small movement of hand and wrist, when we could have talked about loneliness and despair? Why had I pressed him to pick out a fat-tired cart so I could wheel my kayak closer to the water, when I could have asked him how he was doing, whether everything was all right? But you just didn't talk about those things with people you barely knew. Instead you skimmed the surface, talking about things that were tangible. The shape of hulls and how each had their advantages. Rudders versus skegs.

I remembered Moon Reservoir, and a woman with rocks in her backpack. Alaska, after all, wasn't some magic panacea. People were sad everywhere. A boat on the water could not save you, no matter how far you paddled.

Though I didn't know Wyatt well, I could feel the gap he had left behind, the gap all people left behind when they departed. For some, the ragged edges never stitched back together.

I had stayed out as long as I dared, and the ocean had no answers. Even in June, you had to come in sometime. I lingered along the island fringe as long as I could until the sky started wheeling toward darkness. I turned my kayak toward the marina and the uncertainty of home.

As I gained the safety of the breakwater, I realized that the hours of paddling had made the strokes Wyatt taught me automatic. I knew how to back paddle just enough to clear a rock, and when to quarter into the waves. I had even mastered the scull, the stroke that drove me crazy trying to learn. The paddler's box had become routine.

I thought that life could become routine, and maybe Wyatt's had too, a long slog along a rough coast, no islands to break up the monotony, just forward movement as far as a person could see. I would never know what had caused him to pick up the gun, just that the ocean was not enough anymore. I had been foolish to believe it could be.

I reached the small beach and carefully slid the boat to a stop. My face was wet from a mixture of rain and tears. It came to me that I had tamped my emotions down as cleanly as I used to pound dirt down on a trail with a rock bar. It took going far out into the ocean to let them out again. In order to survive the marriage, I had submerged myself far below the sunlit zone, past where any warmth existed. I didn't know whether this was what had happened to Wyatt and to the woman at Moon Reservoir, but it seemed to me that the trouble began when you did this.

I made myself a promise on that beach: to be true to the woman I was out on the sea. I was beginning to be divided in two, between her and someone else whom I became on land. On the sea, I had learned to size up the ocean, pick a point, and head for it, the map fastened on my cockpit. I could carry a rifle and sleep in a tent while bears passed by on their way to the salmon streams. In contrast, the woman I was onshore kept to the corners, swallowed her words. She tiptoed through life convinced she was going to make a mistake. It was getting harder to lead these two separate lives. Soon, I knew, it would be impossible.

I pulled my boat onto the cart, making sure not to scrape its underside more than I already had. There was nobody who could repair it now; I would have to be careful. The days in June were the longest they would ever be. I had plenty of time and yet there didn't seem to be time enough.

I would start small, with something I hoped would be simple. It was time to learn to ride a bike.

three

On Baranof Island, people rode bikes everywhere. Road bikes, mountain bikes, cruiser bikes with baskets. A couple of brave souls even mounted unicycles and swerved down the rain-soaked streets. They left bikes propped outside bars, dragged them onto floatplanes, and carried them on boats to other islands. Drunks stole them, rode them home, and completed the ride of shame the next day to return them to their owners.

People rode through gales, in torrential downpours, and across salmon streams. One rider was even knocked off his bike on the fish hatchery road by a passing brown bear, but he still rode. Bikes in this place were as essential as breathing. Most destinations were within a handful of miles, not worth firing up the car. Many people did not even own cars, or shared vehicles among a group of close-knit friends. Bikes were the way to go.

My husband, an avid rider, had no interest in teaching me. He had perhaps learned his lesson from the rifle debacle. He didn't like riding outside anyway, not fond of rain. He set up a noisy bike trainer in our tiny living room, turning the television to ear-splitting volume. Through summer and winter he rode it, never getting anywhere. Though I could have hopped onto the trainer, I wanted to learn how to go somewhere.

I approached Rowan at the bike tour shop where she led trips for tourists, guiding them as they wavered on two wheels, most of them not having ridden in years. I hesitated before revealing the truth. I had held it close to me for so long, the voice in my head spitting out what felt like the truth: *People are going to laugh at you if you tell. Everybody knows how to ride a bike. Something must be deeply wrong with you if you can't.*

Desire won out. I confessed all in a shameful whisper: "I don't know how to ride a bike," I said, hardly daring to look at her. All along I had pretended that it was lack of wanting rather than ability that had kept me on two feet instead of balancing on two wheels. To me this was a deep, dark secret, one worthy of ridicule, but she only shrugged.

"Plenty of people learn to ride as adults," she said, citing someone we both knew who had recently mastered it. I had no idea he hadn't known how until now: I had seen him just the other day pedaling effortlessly down the Harbor Mountain Road. In her business, she had seen this before. Even the people on her trips could barely ride, hadn't ridden since they were kids. If they could, I could too. I still didn't quite believe this, and as she went to pick out a bike, I almost called to her to forget it. What would be different now from all the other times?

She wheeled out a bike that had seen hard times. A hardtail Trek, it was not a thing of beauty, but it was perfect. I could put my feet flat on the ground when I felt like I was tilting. I couldn't damage the finish any further. Nobody would steal it.

"You have to get some momentum," Rowan said. "It won't work if you're standing still. Keep trying. I've got to get back to the bike shop."

I scanned the old lumberyard like a thief, slow and easy, looking for witnesses. The last thing I wanted was an onlooker. When other kids had graduated from tricycles to training wheels, I had wobbled on a too-large, hand-me-down bike in frustration. Without training wheels, I was unable to find my balance. The truth was, I had always been a kid who gave up when things got hard. I gave up on ballet, gymnastics, softball, and bike riding when the pointe shoes came out, when we had to hang from the uneven bars, when the ball, hurtled by a meaty fifth-grader, came too fast toward my bat. The inner voice told me I wasn't athletic, that I lacked good balance. I believed the voice.

Ever since then, I had been trying to prove it wrong. I had taken on hard things, working as a firefighter and on trail crews. But there was still a small sliver of me that believed that all of that had been a fluke. Riding a bike seemed like the last hurdle. Tiny children could do it. Surely, I could too.

Over the years I had watched my friends swoop in long, lazy circles on their way to trailheads, skis and boards stuffed in backpacks. They went on long rides together, returning windburned and mud spattered. They spoke a language I could not understand, sprinkled with words like derailleur, chain ring, and sprocket. It was a world I only glimpsed from a distance, a country I thought I would never be able to visit.

Sometimes they invited me along, never guessing the truth. I went to great lengths to keep my secret. I'm a runner, I said. Not a bike rider. I don't own a bike. They offered me bikes, rides to the trails, weekends in Moab. I made up excuses and they accepted them, not guessing the real reason. After all, everyone could ride a bike. I was missing out, they said. Maybe next time. They took off without backward glances. I stood, hands stuffed in pockets, watching them ride away. I wasn't one of them, and I knew I never would be.

But maybe I could be now. I placed a tentative foot on a pedal and pushed off. The bike swerved alarmingly and I barely avoided a fall by lunging my feet onto the ground. I straddled the bike, gathering my courage. The next time one pedal made a partial circle, but I couldn't get my other foot up in time. I stuttered across the concrete like a teenager trying to drive a stick shift. Place a foot, push off, bring up the other foot, waver to one side, slap both feet down to avoid a crash.

Long after Rowan had gone home, I continued to wobble on the ancient bike, holding my breath as I glided for a few rotations. Frustrated tears gathered in my eyes as I failed to gain any ground. But each time, I realized, the wheels were turning a little farther before I bailed for safety.

I didn't learn that day, or the day after that. But I knew I would this time. I was going to become a bike rider. Someday I would ride the entire length of this town, the whole fourteen miles, nothing slowing me down.

≈

In my family, water was something you passed through, a means to an end. As a five-year-old, I sat life jacketed and compliant in a wooden canoe, my parents' paddles dipping in unison as we wove through lakes studded with islands, en route to a wilderness campsite. Most nights from my twin bed I heard the lonely call of a foghorn across Lake Superior, a warning to the freighters passing by. When I was in elementary school, a classmate's father succumbed to hypothermia when the family boat was swamped, using the last of his strength to hold his daughter above the water. Unwary college students, drawn to the docks during winter storms, were swept off the breakwater by rogue waves, and sometimes their bodies were never recovered. Then there was the legend of the *Edmund Fitzgerald*, foundering near where I lived, men sent to watery graves. The message was clear: water was deep and unknowable. Better to stay onshore and admire from a distance.

Years later I toed the edge of the junior high school pool, choosing this elective rather than the formidable chorale class, since I could not carry a tune. The water smelled of detergent and churned with the uneven strokes of the kids who already knew something about swimming.

The teacher, a sturdy woman in flip-flops, gestured impatiently. "Swim to the end of the pool!" she hollered.

Another girl and I eyed each other. Wasn't this beginning swimming? How could we swim when we didn't know how? But you didn't disobey a teacher. Instead I hopped in and dog-paddled down the lanes, coughing as I swallowed water, eyes stinging from chlorine. I clung to the wall, breathing hard as I gained on the deep end. "Don't hold on to the wall!" the teacher admonished. "Swim!"

Far behind me, a tiny boy floundered, kicking wildly.

The teacher leaned over the pool as the kid gave up and struggled to the shallow end. He cowered as she approached.

"What are you, retarded?" she boomed. The kid cried quietly. The rest of us shivered by the pool's edge, shrinking from the teacher's critical gaze. After an endless hour of drills, I left the class and never returned. Swimming, I was convinced, was too hard. Not for me.

When I moved to Florida for a few seasons, I tested the ocean, but only as far out as I could stand. This water, the temperature of bathwater, seemed benign, not something that could kill me. Still, I paddled my kayak with caution, never venturing far from land.

Now I knew I had to learn to swim. Too many people died each year from not knowing. Even though the water's chill turned blood to ice in minutes, knowing how to float on it could, perhaps, buy me time. As I paddled my boat forty miles from town, I was uneasily aware that I was taking a big risk. In paddling, as in many other things, you were only as strong as your weakest link. I was also risking the lives of my partners. My graceless dog paddle would not save anyone. I resolved to go to the pool and, at forty years old, learn what I should have long ago.

≈

I went to the ancient pool where we had learned our self-rescues. It was steeped in chlorine, a fog of it hanging over the surface. I could barely see the bottom through the cloudy depths. Venturing to the shallow end, I scanned the pool for anyone who might be watching. The lifeguard slouched in his chair, looking bored. A few people busily stroked back and forth. The length of a lap stretched out before me, much farther than it had appeared in our boats.

I gulped a breath of air and began windmilling my arms and motoring my feet, lifting my head occasionally for a desperate breath. I made it a few feet before I had to stop and cling to the wall. Watching the other swimmers, I pushed off again, trying to copy what they were doing. Finally, I bumped up against the far end. Not daring to look at the lifeguard, I took a moment to breathe. Maybe I was better than I thought. Maybe I could do this swimming thing.

With a wild spray of kicking feet, I regained the starting point, breathing heavily. The thought of another lap seemed impossible. Most of the other swimmers appeared to be absorbed in their own workouts, except for the man in the lane next to me, who, I realized, had observed the entire lap. He wore a Speedo and a look of pity.

I avoided his gaze, hoping he would swim off, but he stayed put. "Oh, you *poor thing*," he said. "You know, I have taught many women *your age* how to swim." When I said nothing, he shrugged, kicked off the edge in a perfect flip turn, and swam away.

I dangled at the edge of the pool for a minute. The other swimmers, surfacing to drink out of their water bottles, cast me curious glances. You didn't come to a pool to just hang out in the shallow end, especially after only one lap. The man who had spoken executed another flip turn at the far end and headed back. I knew I couldn't stand to have him see me struggle for another lap. Giving up, I fled, embarrassed.

A reed-thin woman emerging from the shower stared as I sniffled in the locker room. "Are you OK?" she asked. I nodded, faking a stomachache. The familiar feeling of failure chased me to my car. It had been with me all my life, lurking in the background as I attempted to rush the volleyball net or climb the rope for the President's Fitness Test. Sometimes it had been easier to give up, to slide back to the waiting mat or to pretend nonchalance at every fumble. It had been easier to go back to the things I knew how to do, like run for hours in the forest. The difficult things I had persevered in, like fighting fire, had been hard won, gained only by stubbornness and a natural endurance for suffering that had carried me well past ability.

As I drove in defeat back home, the ocean caught my eye. It was a calm afternoon, the perfect time for paddling. Motorboats stitched across the blue canvas, heading to the fishing grounds or to hunt the slopes of Kruzof Island. A small armada of kayaks, blue, orange, and red, arrowed the passage between Jamestown Bay and the Eastern Channel. Wyatt, I thought, and some clients, but of course Wyatt was long gone; it was someone else.

The ocean was so vast and the boats were so small. From here, far above it, I imagined I could see the different layers of the ocean, the deeper blue where the shallows gave way to the profound, unattainable, light-deprived depths where no human could go. I thought I could see the underwater currents, the rips that formed near Kruzof Island. There was so much left to learn about the ocean, and I would never be able to do it unless I learned how to move through it without the safety of a boat.

I would not give up this time, I thought. I would learn to swim.

I dreaded returning to the critical eyes at the old pool, but fortunately there was another pool at the high school, filled with salt water, not chemicals. A master's class had begun and I crept in with misgivings.

"I don't really know how to swim," I admitted to the others, who were armed with tools of the trade: kickboards, swim buoys, or clawlike paddles they placed on their hands to create drag. Some of them even had their favorite lanes. They guarded them jealously against all comers, lining up at the doors to race in early, unshowered, to place their props near the diving boards. Any prospective lane sharers had to wait timidly for these experts to rise for air midlap and blurt out, "Can I share this lane?" in the brief seconds before a flip turn.

Most of the people did not need any lessons. Former competitive swimmers, they raced down the lanes with explosive speed. They rose out of the water like whales, executing the hardest stroke of all, the butterfly. They swam entire lengths underwater, propelled with only the smallest of kicks. They were fish, and I was some kind of land creature, unadapted to water.

But they were welcoming and taught me what they knew. As I backstroked, sputtering from water to the face, one woman showed me how to kick, a lithe and seamless movement, instead of the desperate lunging I had been doing. Less was more, they told me. You didn't have to fight the water like I was doing. Another demonstrated how to breathe on both sides of the body, instead of just one. Because I was new, they said, I could learn the right way, not be burdened with the old habits they were trying to shake.

To my surprise and probably everyone else's, I stuck with it. Our eighteen-year-old instructor paced the edge of the pool, giving me advice. I had to own my body in the water, I gathered. Instead of floating like a log, flat and unyielding, swimming was all about curving to meet the least resistance. Your body was constantly in motion, one hand reaching far overhead, the other one poised to go.

I felt entire muscles loosen as I swam, unfurl themselves from the clenched hold I had held them in for years. I pictured a ball of yarn slowly unraveling with each stroke I took.

I was still the slowest to get to the end of the pool, and I never finished the drills our instructor wrote on the dry erase board. I could manage only an approximation of the butterfly down half the lap before succumbing to a lazy dolphin kick. When the lanes were full and we had to circle swim, three people to a lane in a roundabout motion, I often had to redline through the lap as fast as I could in a desperate attempt to stay in the rotation.

For the remainder of the season, the good swimmers still claimed their favorite lanes early, guarding their rectangle of water with the vigilance of eagles at a salmon stream. An interloper, I slunk in shyly, inserting myself into the mix. Soon I had my own favorite lane.

There were times when I almost got it. As I sliced through the lane, keeping an eye on the thick black line that marked my boundary, sometimes stroke and kick aligned so that I shot forward as if propelled by a force outside my own making. At those moments, the bass from the music our instructor played on the overhead speakers a muffled thump, I thought I came closer to narrowing the gap between water and body.

In my boat, I felt as if I understood water more now that I could swim through it. In my bulky dry suit, I would be more of an anchor than a fish, but I could imagine kicking free of rubber boots and making it to shore with the strokes I had practiced. Learning to swim changed the way I saw the ocean. It was no longer an adversary I had to outwit but a companion.

t rescue

There is no place for independence in a T rescue, but it is the best way to get back in a capsized boat. The person in the water hangs on wherever she can, maneuvering her craft so it is perpendicular to the upright paddler. The person who is safe must draw the flooded boat across her bow, flipping it over to drain the water. Then she pulls the boat parallel and stabilizes it as the castaway climbs in.

You find out how selfish you really are if you have to attempt a T. Every cell in your body is screaming for you to save yourself. After all, you are safe. It is not you who has made the mistake; it is not you who is in trouble. By attempting a T, you are putting yourself in real danger. This is when you learn what kind of stuff you are made of.

one

To do a T rescue you had to depend on someone else. I wasn't used to that. I had learned early on that I could really depend only on myself. As a wildland firefighter I had to rely on my crew to save my life if things went bad, but I was expected to carry my own load, even if the guys outweighed me by a hundred pounds. You didn't ask for help unless the situation was dire, or unless an extra pair of hands was clearly needed to contain a stubborn blaze. Presented with hose to roll or water containers to carry, you were expected to cowboy up and do it. Your value lay in how much you could carry, how fast you could hike, how long you could hang in there on the night shifts with trees falling silently all around you. I didn't want anyone to depend on me either.

In a T, I couldn't stay in my own boat and paddle on by. It took courage to pull a swamped kayak onto mine in rough seas, flip it over, and then drop it back in the water. I was uneasily aware of how unstable this made my own boat. A panicked person could tug too hard, pulling me over with them. Often, Wyatt had explained, the rescuer had to calm down the person in the water, talk them through the steps. This took guts in a big ocean. But it could be done. In the worst case, you had to know when to quit, when a rescue was impossible. That was the hardest decision of all.

I tried again and again in class, pulling people I had just met from their deliberate capsizes. Couldn't we just do the self-rescue? I thought with impatience. My boat wobbled dangerously as the person I was supposed to save clung onto my stern for dear life. Couldn't they just go overturn their own boat? Why endanger the rest of us?

But practicing the T, I began to see that you did not always have to go it alone. You could be a team against the things the sea threw at you. It was much easier to get back in your boat with someone steadying it than to do it on your own. It occurred to me that I had never wanted to rely on someone because I had never been sure I was someone, in turn, who could be relied on. The responsibility had seemed too great. What if I let them down, let them slip under the surface? What if I wanted to move on, the way I always had?

In my old life, I had begrudgingly accepted the earnest interns who wanted to be wilderness rangers. I had tolerated their lapses in judgment, the wild, untutored swings of their Pulaskis.

At the same time, I had agonized over exposing them to lightning-touched ridges and waist-deep rivers. Leading a squad into a wildfire was equally hazardous. Rookies, mesmerized by flame or bored by inaction, vanished on quests of their own and had to be rounded up. Would they recognize the subtle signs that could lead to a firestorm? Were they fast enough to escape? Each step, with someone else depending on me for the answers, seemed fraught with grave consequences.

When we had learned how to do the T to Wyatt's satisfaction, we had rinsed the kayaks with a hose outside the building and loaded them in his trailer for transport. Wet hair turning frosty in the winter air, I headed for my truck and home. I pondered what I had just learned. I was starting to think that each kayak stroke had lessons that could be applied to life.

Maybe, I thought, if I stopped trying to turn my husband into a different man, if I stopped wanting him to rescue me from the mistakes of my past, we could rescue each other.

In the kitchen, my husband was angry. It didn't matter why. He was angry a lot of the time, a slow, simmering rage at people he thought had wronged him, at the circumstances that had placed him here in the rain forest, at me for keeping him here. Anger was the only emotion he would allow to show.

"It's always your way!" he yelled, throwing a bar stool. It clattered near my feet. I had no idea what transgression I had made, but I had learned it was better to stand down, disappear for a while. Though he was not violent, my husband was like a gale. He stormed through the house muttering curses until he blew himself out. With temerity, I had once suggested medication. I thought the anger was a stand-in for the real cause, a deep depression he was trying to beat back.

"You know how hard it was for me to quit alcohol," he raged, infuriated at the mere suggestion of chemicals. Seething, he stomped from the room. I gave up, after that taking note of when storm clouds were gathering and making myself scarce.

I knew I had gales of my own. Sometimes loneliness drove me to desperate tears that I tried to save for the shower. I wanted too much from him, he said; he just could not give it. Our house was a stormy sea, never at rest. I dreamed of the ways I could truly vanish: a note on the table, an early morning ferry. None of these seemed quite fair. Those choices would be running away. I was good at running away; I had proven this all my life. This time, I knew, I had to face it. On an island, surrounded by big water, that was what you did.

Sometimes, too, people didn't want to be rescued. I thought of the woman at Moon Reservoir, of Wyatt. I remembered that a drowning person sometimes struggled with the rescuer, convinced the rescuer was preventing him from reaching safety. Sometimes, too, T rescues didn't work, despite everything you tried. The waves might be too big, the wind too strong. Still, Wyatt had said, his shy grin lighting up his face, you had to try. You couldn't just leave someone out there in the big ocean when you had the means to save them. One thing Wyatt hadn't been able to teach us was when you gave up. He implied that you never did. Even as the waves dragged both boats out to the open, unbroken sea, you kept attempting the T. There was no reason to stop until you finally decided there was no use.

But how did you know? I asked him. It seemed like there should be a formula, steps to follow. But there wasn't. It was something, Wyatt had said, that was different for everyone. Something you just had to decide for yourself.

two

In September, a DeHavilland Beaver float plane disappeared. The color of ocean and sky, it was last seen overhead in Peril Strait by passengers on the Alaska Marine ferry, last heard by a couple working the herring fishery miles downcoast. It vanished just like a snap of the fingers, the forest and ocean zipping up tight behind it. One minute it was flying low, two hundred feet above the water, trying to beat the storm. The next minute it was gone.

Chance and I flew through shifting clouds, looking for a sign. It was not a good day to fly and we were scud running, ducking under low-lying fog and dodging the squalls in an uneven zigzag, trying to find better air. We didn't say it, but it looked like we might have to turn back.

It was fall in coastal Alaska and on cue the rains shouldered in, pushing their way across Baranof Island in a dense band. Storms lined up in the Gulf one after another, like shots in a rifle. Fog hugged the mountains. Gales swept across the ocean, whipping the waves to twenty-five feet and higher. We were on the downward slide toward October, the daylight turning stingy. It was a bad time to be out.

We were all out anyway: skiffs poured down Olga Strait looking for broken-off floats or debris. Hikers from the mountain search-and-rescue team bashed through the forest on compass bearings. Planes like ours skimmed the valleys, flying as low as the pilots dared. It seemed like the whole town was out searching for people they didn't even know. I liked that about this place. If you were in trouble, someone would come looking.

≈

This was the truth I punched down like bread dough every time I pushed off from shore: there was no way to be truly safe. Big ocean, gales, bears—

this was a place that could knock you on your ass. Here you could truly disappear. Most often those who vanished were never found. A handful of times their dogs survived instead, half-starved Labradors found on some unnamed island. Sometimes there were clues, sometimes not.

On my kayak patrols we carried radios in our boats, but there were dead spots back in the long, dark fjords where the sheer rock walls blocked signals. Even satellite phones crackled in and out of range, leaving us in midsentence. Cell service was sketchy even in town. Out there, you were truly on your own. It was both exhilarating and terrifying. Every decision I made, whether to paddle that day or stay onshore, what clothes to wear, even where to camp, could add up to surviving or not. It all added up to a heightened alertness. Unlike ever before, I was keenly aware of the feel of rain on my cheek, the direction of the wind.

Sometimes, standing onshore, I debated for hours: Go or not? I paced the cobble beach, trying to read the wind and waves. I thumbed up the marine forecast on the radio, searching for answers in the flat, emotionless recording. It often seemed like a gamble, a toss of the dice. What I saw from shore could be very different out in the ocean.

September was a bad month to disappear. It was an unsettled and murky time, when things could go either way. Sometimes after weeks of rain the ocean turned flat and beguiling, the winds calm, seducing you out far from shore. Other times the gales stalled over the island. The forecasts were often unreliable. I had been stuck out for days in September, waiting for a floatplane to come back.

The plane had taken off two days before, Eric at the controls. Four tourists had crowded in after him with their rain jackets and their new rubber boots and their fishing rods. They never made it to their destination, Baranof Warm Springs, on the other side of the island. It was only fifteen miles away, a jumble of peaks, glaciers, and bottomless lakes. You could hike it, if you had good knees and an iron will. But you couldn't usually fly it in September. Instead you had to take the long way, fifty miles around by the ocean.

≈

The last time I saw Eric, a month before and a hundred miles from where Chance and I were searching now, he had bounced on his heels on the floats of his plane, waiting to pick me up. A smile split his face as he saw who his passenger was. "You're everywhere!" he yelled over the sound of the prop. It was true; my job with the Forest Service took me to isolated bays and deserted lakes, and it was usually he or one of the other pilots who took me, ruffling the water as we landed in one remote place or another. Planes stitched through the sky in this part of Alaska; we all turned our faces upward like flowers, knowing who flew them by the color of the underbelly and by their grace in an uncertain sky. Everyone flew a little differently, and after a time we got to know this. We knew who would risk a crosswind landing and who would turn back, leaving us stuck out in the woods until the next day. We knew who would land on a lake the size of a postage stamp and who wouldn't. We knew who would stay on the beach and who would fly, even in the teeth of a gale.

The pilots all had opinions. Down at the float dock, doing preflights, they talked among themselves in the language of the sky. Forrest, with forty years of flying under his belt, thought that the Beaver had cartwheeled into Deadman's Reach. "If you're flying just above the deck, you don't have time to recover," he said. "The wind slaps you down and you're underwater." Usually Forrest was full of flying stories, tales of drama and risk, but today he was drained of cheer. Chance was the same. A lanky sixty-year-old who had survived a heart attack, he typically brimmed over with joy for life. Today he was silent, somehow older.

In town the rest of us had debated in the grocery store and bars.

"They're under fifty feet of water. They'll never be found."

"No, they're on land somewhere. The psychic said she saw a plane on Catherine Island. Somebody should check Catherine Island."

"Eric's cell phone keeps ringing. Doesn't that mean it's not underwater?"

"Remember the time Forrest flew up Hoggatt Bay thinking it was Red Bluff? That could have happened to them."

"Maybe they're just waiting it out on the beach. It's possible. You know we've been stuck out that long in the fall."

On the ground, Chance talked as easily as a river, but in the air, he dried up to the minimum. He offered few theories.

≈

Every year, someone in town died at the indifferent hands of the wilderness. It was easy to see why. The mountains we flew over were coated in snow most of the year, cloaked in a jungle of slick vegetation below that. The ocean could whip into a frenzy of froth and steep waves in minutes. There was no softness, no quarter given for the foolish or unlucky. Here, the main impression I got was indifference.

There were reminders of planes that had gone down scattered across our island, a litany of crash sites. We had hiked to a crumpled shell at Cold Storage Lake and seen parts of a wing at both Lake Diana and Rust Lake. There were many more planes that had never been found.

≈

Today we had been flying for an hour without any success. The mountains were keeping their own secrets. Cloaked in clouds, they refused to let us in.

"I need a break," Chance said. He landed the plane in Rodman Bay, water foaming in our wake. We opened the doors and gulped wet air as the plane floated in the lumpy ocean. We peed off the floats with our backs to each other. A southwest swell from Chatham Strait pushed toward the shore and a sheet of rain moved through, soaking our fleece jackets. The ceiling was low, ragged scraps of cloud brushing the water. It was lonely standing on the floats, the forest a misty outline. It felt like there was nobody else in the world but us.

"Weather's coming down," Chance said. We scrambled back in our seats. It was raining harder now. Drops streaked across the windshield, an opaque barrier. It was hard to tell water from land; it was all painted the same shade of gray.

Our grid had taken us forty miles to the Duffield Peninsula, a long, forested snout of land that was the most likely route across the island if the mountains weren't clear. We didn't know whether Eric had taken this route. We were only guessing.

We flew over Duffield, back and forth in a slow arc. Somewhere below us in the dense forest there were searchers, but we couldn't spot them. The forest had swallowed them up completely.

I saw death every day as I pushed my kayak paddle through the water. In Port Banks, silver salmon flung themselves over and over at a waterfall, most not making it. They were dying as they swam, their skin turning dull, their eyes milky. Long, curved bones of a doe, winterkill, lay scattered on a beach. Crosses stood on remote beaches. These were the grim souvenirs of a place where the line between life and death was very thin.

We all tried to minimize this with our own rituals. Every year a minister came down to bless the commercial fleet. A list of names was read, those who had been lost at sea. Each had its own story. The boat found circling, nobody on board, a life vest unworn on a hot day. A skiff caught broadside to the waves, both men able to get survival suits on, but one of them slipping away just as they heard the helicopter approach. Another who fell off a dock and was unable to climb back up, the water taking his life in minutes.

Sometimes the people you loved didn't come back. A stumble on slippery deer cabbage high on a mountain, an unexpected wind on the ocean and they were gone. It seemed more frightening to love someone who might not come back, easier to hesitate and draw a curtain over your heart. Back where I had come from, I had no such awareness; the people I had helped carry out of the wilderness there had made obvious errors. I could list them as we heaved each backboard. Trusting a green horse. Not replacing electrolytes. Running a river that demanded more respect. It was easy to tell myself that I would never make those mistakes, and neither would anyone I knew, despite ample evidence to the contrary. Here in Alaska I still wavered, unsure of how deep to dive in.

On one pass I saw something gleaming on a steep slope. "Over there," I said, and Chance turned the plane. We circled and I squinted, wanting to turn the white rock into something else.

"Nothing. Just a rock."

I was unsettled: What if I had missed something? There was so much to see; surely a plane could be hidden deep in the forest. Entire houses did not show up; even people onshore could be missed. I knew that from my own floatplane trips. Often, we even had to throw rocks into the ocean as the pilot circled so he could determine the difference between what he thought he saw and what was there.

By summer, the trees would have new growth, blotting out any signs. Sea currents could tumble a plane end over end, sending it miles along the deep ocean floor. Time could churn on, the forgetting beginning too soon.

I was aware that these were the golden hours, the magic time between when people were found safely or not at all. The clock in my head ticked on with an inescapable urgency.

Five hundred feet below us, the ocean was constricted by islands, narrowed down like a thick muscle. It was more like river than sea. In Sergius Narrows, the tide flowed through so strongly that the buoys marking the route were bent over flat. The state ferry had to stop and drift sometimes, waiting for slack. The names of the waterways we flew over were ominous: Deadman's Reach, Poison Cove, Peril Strait. The monikers reflected things that had happened here centuries ago, events that had become legend. Many of these stories ended in cliffhangers, no resolution.

We talked about the stories of lost mariners in the night over our beach campfires, analyzing their mistakes, trying to shield ourselves from their fate. It was easier to judge than to admit it could happen to us. "He was an accident waiting to happen," we pronounced. "Why wasn't he wearing a life vest? Didn't they check the forecast?"

Another plane had made it to Baranof Warm Springs that day. It was marginal, the winds high, the visibility low, the pilot reported, but doable. It was easy to second-guess.

I kept expecting to see someone waving us down, or a piece of wreckage, some signpost to show that people could not simply vanish. Below us, though, there was only water and trees, a monotonous backdrop of dark blue and lighter green. Occasionally another plane crossed our path, on the same mission. Chance talked quietly to the other pilots, exchanging information about where we had been and what we had not seen. Boats left foaming wakes on the channels. A large cruise ship lumbered at half the speed. The orange Coast Guard helicopter beetled across our path, heading north.

Chance's plane was bright orange too, a color with one purpose. Planes that were blue or green, like the one we were looking for, blended in with the landscape. We could fly right over it and never see it.

"We're looking for sheared-off trees," Chance told me over the intercom. "Look for oil slicks on the water." He paused. "If you see a flock of ravens, let me know." For the last, I didn't need to even ask. I scanned the shores for pieces of airplane floats. My eyes hurt from looking so hard. The whole country sprawled out before me. It was enormous and steep, wild beyond belief.

We looped over Catherine Island in the faint hope that they might have made it this far. I could tell Chance wanted to turn back. He knew what I didn't want to admit, that every sighting had proven to be a dead end. That sleeping bag found floating wasn't theirs. The oil slick on the water was gone when searchers reached it. The white thing on the beach turned out to be a piece of a boat, left over from someone else's tragedy.

I stole a glance at Chance. I couldn't read his face. I thought that he must have his own survival stories; anyone who had lived here long enough did.

A friend told me about buddies who, because of weight, were left behind on a riverbank, the pilot never returning to pick them up. "They built a raft and floated to the nearest town," he said. He matter-of-factly related another story of a plane crash where he and his companions, unscathed, had sat it out for fourteen days on a pass before being spotted. "Luckily we had the caribou I shot," he said. It was his third crash. He still flew.

We all did, putting our faith in small planes and the pilots who flew them. It was the best way to get around, nimbler than boats and cheaper than helicopters. We flew to put out fires, to meetings, and to cabins. We flew to beachside weddings and to memorial services. We joked with the pilots; shared soggy sandwiches and showed them the secrets we found: pictographs smeared on a rock face, ancient cabins slumbering in the weeds. They were our adopted family, united in the face of this indifferent wilderness.

"I'm going back. Fuel," Chance said.

I took one last look, begging the clouds to lift. They didn't.

Chance banked the plane and we headed toward town. Lights shone dimly through the mist as we got closer. "Sterile cockpit," Chance said, reminding me not to talk while he was landing. We taxied to the dock in silence.

It felt sort of like failure, coming back empty. We unloaded in cold rain. Forrest was back too. He shook his head. "Deadman's Reach," he said. Nobody had seen anything, not that day, the day after that, or any of the days after.

The memorial service was bittersweet, with no answers. It was at the outdoor pavilion, and people brought food. A few spoke haltingly, but the truth seemed too large for words. One day you could be here, the next you were gone.

We stared out at the dark ocean. The pungent wilderness pressed in on us from all sides. Our bonfire was all that kept it out. But I knew we would go out again, as we always did. We would take our rifles, and our survival suits, and our carefully protected hearts. We would carry a little spark of hope with us, the hope that we would one day make it back to a home we knew.

three

As soon as we paddled out from the shelter of Klag Bay, I knew I had made a possibly dangerous mistake, one I could not undo.

Twelve-foot waves, steel gray, rolled in from the open ocean, unimpeded in their journey from Japan. Towering over our heads, they tossed our kayaks like toys as we plowed forward toward the sanctuary of the Baird Islands, hulking shadows three miles to the south. Each wave loomed impossibly high, with a roar that filled the entire world. For a few heart-beats, the wave was all there was. It covered everything—the sky, the land, any hope that I had left.

Next to me, Helga's dandelion-blonde head vanished in the wide-bottomed troughs and reappeared high above on the crests of the waves. For brief moments she was suspended three stories above me, digging her paddle into the wave crest for all she was worth. A pair of sea lions chased after her, fascinated by her yellow boat.

She did not meet my glance. This was survival, all of a sudden. We were on our own. The simple steps of a T rescue—draw one boat over the other's bow and flip it to shake out the water while the capsized paddler pushes down on the stern, then stabilize the boat so she can climb in—seemed impossible now, out here in this swirling ocean. How could I have believed in the hope of rescue?

I glanced over at a possible take-out, a small indentation in Slocum Arm with a slice of beach, but going in was impossible: huge rollers pounded the overhanging cliffs. We would be tossed in those waves, smashed up, killed maybe. Turning around, returning to Klag, broadside to the waves, could flip the boats. There was no other choice but to continue on.

I realized that we were in possibly the worst place we could be, wide open and slammed by the southern swell. This was what was called a fetch, an open distance where wind and waves could move freely without encountering land. I remembered the hours at the pool and in the bay, heaving myself in my sloshing cockpit. In the pool there were no real consequences. The water was warm and my feet grazed the bottom.

"Remember, your boat is unstable with all the water in it," Wyatt had yelled, reminding us to use our bilge pumps and quit clowning around. Here in the real thing, I could not picture being able to right a flipped kayak, much less get in it. I could imagine only clinging to the hull, being swept toward the waiting rocks.

As we neared the points, the places where rocks extended spiny fingers out into the ocean, we were in what I called the washing machine: waves bouncing off the cliffs and colliding with the rest of the swell. The sea was confused here, a mass of energy with no place to go. I braced like Wyatt had taught me, slapping my paddle flat against the water, seeking stability. The sky let loose, an icy rain dropping visibility to near zero. This felt like disappearing. It felt like we were about to vanish the way so many others had, our boats filling with water, our fingers slowly losing purchase on the hulls, our bodies tumbling deep into the currents that lay beneath the ocean's surface. We would likely never be found.

I called on Gertrude, my burly half, but she was nowhere to be found. She had vanished sometime in the last year; it was as if she had decided I no longer needed her. I should have been glad, because that meant I had come a long way, but it felt very much like I was on my own.

From somewhere in a place I had forgotten, I summoned up the girl I had once been, a girl who marched through life nearly fearless. I gulped in a breath of clean, salty air. Along with it I took in a thought. I knew I didn't want to be afraid anymore. Not of being alone, not of bears, not of the ocean, not of heartbreak.

I looked ahead at the swirling mass of ocean left to be crossed. I could continue to let fear guide me or I could let it go, finally. Either way, we would make it to safety or we wouldn't. Without the fear, I could finally be free.

I began to laugh as I paddled. I sang snippets of songs to drown out the pounding of the waves. "Wild thing!" I howled. "You make my heart sing!"

The swell was no less rough, the situation no less dire. I had been the one to change.

After an hour, two hours, some unmeasurable amount of time, we paddled into safer waters. It was almost disappointing to be finished with the storm.

The water calmed to a ripple inside the protection of the Baird Islands. Across the water, ruffled now with diminishing whitecaps, the long mouth of Slocum Arm was swallowed up in the fog.

I pulled into a small bay where I had camped before and motioned to Helga. We beached our boats carefully on the cobble and began the complicated unloading process that we now knew by heart. We reached far inside the hatch covers, piling gear up by our feet, moving it as the tide advanced. By now, seven years in, this unloading was automatic. I briefly remembered the younger woman I had been on my first kayak patrol, shivering on a beach, surrounded by too much gear, starting from zero.

Don't be so afraid, I wanted to tell her. You can make it on your own, the way you always have. Don't marry a man whose heart is frozen, impossible to thaw. Don't break yourself like a wave against the rocks.

I pulled the rifle out of the cockpit and slid open the magazine to insert the fat golden shells. I slung it over my shoulder as we hiked through the wet grass, the cuffs of our rain pants sticking to our ankles, soaked through. There were no bears today; we were safe.

We held the tarp on opposite ends, wrestling with it as the wind sneaked underneath. It billowed, nearly escaping as Helga tied her end to a tree and I followed suit on mine, running the parachute cord along its length to keep it taut. We pitched our tents beneath it, sinking the pegs deep into the loam of the forest floor.

The rain was a staccato drumbeat as we crouched over our camp stove, stirring a sluggish pot of potato soup. We set our extra pots out to catch the rain. The nearest freshwater was a murky stream a half-mile paddle down the scalloped hem of the island, and neither of us could face it tonight.

After dinner, we sat under our tarp. There were no other people, no lights, no sound but the thunder of waves on the outer edge of our island, the part that took the full punch of the sea. I could feel my body unwrapping itself, the layers of anger and fear and sadness falling away with each unconstrained breath.

I glanced over at Helga, sitting with the sleeves of her wool sweater pulled down over her hands. I wanted to ask her whether being married felt lonelier than each one of her single days, alone on an open road like I had been. I wanted to tell her about the way my husband and I passed each other in the hallway, not touching, each of us our own planet.

But I didn't. We had been over this ground before and there was nothing new to say. Helga, much more pragmatic than I, knew that if you were in an impossible situation, you found a way out. You didn't pace the beach waiting for someone to rescue you. You took matters into your own hands.

Instead I flipped on the marine radio, listening for the automated voice that intoned the coastal forecast. Rain, heavy at times, it droned. Winds to twenty knots. Seas, fourteen feet.

I squinted across to Slocum Arm, but inside the protection of Smooth Channel, it was impossible to tell what gales were building out on the open ocean.

"Captain Johnny might not be able to get around Klokachef Island," I said. "We might be out here a few extra days."

Helga shrugged. This wasn't her first rodeo. I settled back down on the pebble beach. Since the first time I had been stuck out, I had relaxed a lot more about the possibility. We always brought extra food. We told others back at home not to wait up for us. I viewed these days as bonus ones, time to hunker in place, take short walks across the small islands that confined us. It was sometimes an unwelcome surprise when our rescuers hove into view.

Though I didn't mention it to Helga, I knew that I had put us both in danger today. We could have scrapped the trip, stayed back in town and waited out the gale that I could clearly see in the forecast. We could have stayed in Klag Bay where only a minor swell would force its way in. Though Helga took our desperate paddle in stride, I knew that I was taking more and more chances. Being out here, even in the face of a storm that could have taken our lives, was preferable to being at home.

≈

A pair of bald eagles perched in a tree near our camp, carefully studying the water. I looked where they were watching but could see nothing. Probably the opaque bodies of salmon were swimming deep below, bound for the rivers where they were born.

As I sat there, I remembered how it had felt to battle the waves. There had been a moment when I was weightless, poised on the crest of each wave. I also knew that it had been foolish to take on the sea the way I had. I pictured the consequences: one or both of us capsized, drowned or perhaps making it to a rocky shore, the paperwork that would ensue, the guilt that would overcome the survivor, the unanswerable questions. I had done this in order to run away from what faced me on land. It was one thing to be brave, another to be reckless.

The next realization hit me like a slap of water in the face. My husband was using the tools he had to run away too. He surrounded himself with constant noise, volume turned as high as it could go, to drown whatever critical voice piped up in his own head. To escape from the reality that we were running as fast as we could in opposite directions. Because, like me, he knew somehow, deep in the deepest part of himself, that it was too late.

≈

The last day of our kayak trip, we waited on the beach for Captain Johnny's boat to chug into sight. We had paddled for four days in unceasing rain, recording the condition of old fox farms with their sagging sheds and chicken wire, remnants of a brief fur industry. We had found illegal cabins and posted the date of their impending demise, a ninety-day requirement so that the owners could come gather up their effects. We had marked down campsite locations on our maps and picked up trash left behind. It was time to go home, or at least to figure out where home would be.

Our gear was packed back in the dry bags, the kayaks readied for transport, and there was nothing to do but watch. It was a dynamic, ever-changing scene. Nothing stayed the same for long. The tide crept in, inch by inch, a difference of fifteen, sometimes twenty feet from the low. Beaches disappeared under the endless slow churn of water. This land was still rebounding from the thumb of the glaciers. North of here, it bounced back as much as an inch per year. After deglaciation, only a blink of time ago, we would have seen open pine forests instead of this patchwork of Sitka spruce, hemlock, and cedar. Things changed so fast up here that I could never find my balance.

≈

Captain Johnny made it through, shaking salt spray off his curly hair. He hollered that it was touch and go out there by Klokachef and that we'd better get a move on. We loaded the boats in double time, strapping them securely to the outside rails, and handed gear in a conga line to the back deck. Finally, I stepped on just as he gunned it for a quick escape.

The boat shuddered through the chop, past the submerged rocks of Piehle Passage, the dazzling green expanse of the place we called the Potato Patch for the old Tlingit gardens that used to flourish there. I sat in the wheelhouse taking it all in: the broad back of Chichagof Island, its peaks now colored brilliant emerald, the ever-changing ocean restless along the gravel beaches. I saw the dark shapes of bears in the estuaries and the steep bights where water washed in and out in an unceasing rhythm.

"This is my home," Captain Johnny said. His expansive gesture took in the gray whales feeding along the rocks, the eagles perched like ornaments in a lone hemlock, the pink flamingos some joker once set out in the trees. He turned the boat toward town, a grin on his face.

As the rounded cone of Mount Edgecumbe came into view, Johnny pointed out the tourists swarming the cruise ships looming over town. "They lead miserable lives compared to us," he said. "Can you imagine? Indiana?"

Neither of us said anything. Indiana might be nice; my ancestors had come from there, but I didn't want to live there.

We glided past the familiar landmarks: the small mound of Guide Island, the white buildings of the fish camp at Dog Point. The long stretch of beach where surfers in wet suits took on the swells. It suddenly all seemed dear and familiar, now that I was thinking about leaving. This suddenly felt like the closest to home I had ever been.

roll

Though there is some disagreement among historians as to whether the Aleut and Inuit hunters used the roll, with some asserting that they were too skilled to have to roll in the first place, there is no question that people have been rolling their boats for decades. To do a kayak roll, a better term for this maneuver, first you have to be in a boat that fits. If the fit is sloppy, you will be unable to execute the flick of your hips that is essential for righting your boat.

First you lean into the water until you capsize. Kiss the deck of the boat and push your paddle forward to begin a big sweep from bow to stern. As you do this, straighten your body and flick your hips to smoothly roll upright.

You have to commit to the roll, and most people lose their nerve halfway. Suspended underwater, trapped in their spray skirts, their mind begins to panic. Though rolls are mostly for whitewater, and most paddlers will tell you that it is difficult to right a fully loaded sea kayak, this maneuver allows you to stay in the boat rather than drop into freeing water with uncertain waves. It is always far easier to stay in what is known than to commit to the sea, though it may not seem like it at the time.

Though it also seems like you have gotten nowhere with the roll, brought yourself back up to the same old sea state you were in before, in essence you have taken the power back from the ocean. You are in charge, at least for now.

one

I had come to Alaska thinking I could learn everything, but I was realizing that there would always be more to know. Staying put in one place didn't have to be ordinary like I had always thought. A well-loved piece of ground still held surprises. I had never stayed in one spot long enough to know that. In some, I had barely lasted one season, not long enough to see anything.

Gales sometimes took me by surprise. It often seemed that there had been no signs to predict their arrival, but looking back later, I could see there had been. Even as I paddled through Sitka Sound, the slurp of my paddle loud in the morning hush, I realized later that there had been clues. A small, determined breeze ruffled the cedars lining the shore. The bell in the buoy clanged lazily, signaling a change in the swell. I may have noticed these, but I saw what I wanted to see.

But there was a part of me that loved the gales. On the days when extreme weather swept the straits, I stared, mesmerized. Wind bent the pine trees flat and whipped the sea into a froth of white. Gales always blew themselves out eventually, just as if they were exhausted by their own ferocity.

"I can't do this anymore," I told my husband. It was April, the month when things started to turn around. Daylight increased by several minutes each morning and the rain fell off sharply, leaving us with a string of sunlight that almost seemed like it would stay forever. You could stand anything in April, I had always thought, but I was wrong.

I had intended to wait to leave until I had a plan in place, carefully thought out and executed. I would leave gracefully, leaving hearts intact. In the end, my loneliness chose for me. I knew I could not face another winter like the ones before. I could not face even another summer, though summers were the best times of all.

≈

Gales could kill you if you weren't prudent. Every year somebody got caught, hadn't run for shore when they should have. Even survival suits couldn't save you in a churning sea. They should have known, people said when the news hit town of someone else lost. But I knew better: sometimes it was worth the risk. Sometimes you kept going into a certain storm because there was no other alternative. You could sit it out on the beach, but not forever.

His lips thinned in anger and his eyes blazed with a cold fire. His rage was like hail hitting me, leaving a sting with each word.

You need professional help.

You never tried to fit in with my family.

You had an agenda all along.

I let the words break over me without speaking. There was nothing left to say. We each had lived different versions of our stories.

He sat, deflated, on the bed.

This was where he would tell me he was willing to do anything, I thought. That he did not want to lose me. It might not be too late after all. Maybe we could reach back to the older days, hiking together on the rounded spine of the island, waiting for a floatplane to come get us. Maybe there was still hope before breaking apart.

"What am I going to do with the rest of my life?" he asked instead, and my heart sank. *His life?* It had never been our life. Later he told friends that this had come out of nowhere, like lightning striking from a pale blue sky. He had not seen the signs, although to me they had been a clear warning of what was to come.

I had tried long enough.

I fled the house I had bought and sought refuge in a friend's vacant apartment. For the first time in years, I felt myself unfolding from a clenched fist. There was no undercurrent of anger that simmered below the surface. There was no wondering which man I would find at home, the one I had fallen for or the new one, whom I could not recognize. I did not have to be timid, wondering whether I was saying or doing the right thing. I did not have the concert of two voices, merging in their critical assessment of who I was.

≈

Gales always left lingering aftereffects. After a storm, Helga and I found driftwood thicker than our forearms, tossed high into the woods by a powerful force. We found pieces of ships half buried in sand. Our former campsites even changed, trees uprooted and toppled over where our tents had once stood. Even long after the wind had exhausted itself, I could see where it had been.

I knew it would be the same for us. You couldn't walk away from a marriage, even a short one like ours, without some scars. Even if we recovered, rolled ourselves back up for another stab at life, we would carry what had happened to us forever.

I felt the weight of this settle around me, as dense as the fog. There were many nights I sat on the kitchen floor, the only place that felt good and solid, a tsunami of regret and despair overcoming me until I could not move from there for hours.

How had it come to this? I had been so sure that this was the end, the place and the person I would end up beside. I had missed clues in him, and I had disregarded clues in myself. Together we had created a gale from which it was impossible to recover.

≈

This was how it ended, not in the wilderness but in a courtroom. It was hard to breathe, as if something heavy sat on my chest. There were no windows, but I sensed the rain. It was late fall now, the turning of the seasons, the hardest time of all.

My husband and I sat close enough to touch, but we didn't. We hadn't touched in months. I had seen him only in passing as we carried paperwork between government floors. We had avoided each other's gaze.

The judge asked each of us in turn whether we had irreconcilable differences. He looked bored; he probably saw this every day.

Both of us said yes in an eerie re-creation of our wedding vows years earlier. The judge yawned. *But I tried,* I wanted to say. I wanted to give him a list of the ways it hadn't worked, something to show that we weren't the same as people who just gave up. But we were those people.

Earlier we had filled out the paperwork stating how we would separate our belongings. We owned very little of value, and it was laid out starkly on the paper: two pickups, ten years old. A boat. The house, in my name, my down payment, money I had scraped up from years of seasonal work—but my husband now had claim to half the value. My bank account, twice the size of his when we married, merged with his meager one at his insistence, now half his. I would leave the marriage poorer than when I went in. For the most part, though, our belongings were still separate. It showed me how divided we had always been.

In the end, there was so little to divide. Like separate countries, we had kept our boundaries intact, not intersecting. My truck. My boat. My heart.

≈

There was an uncomfortable silence as the judge studied our paperwork. I knew our divorce would be recorded in the town newspaper in black and white, our failure out there for everyone to see. We worked in the same building, where it was impossible to avoid each other, and our coworkers gave us a wide berth, perhaps fearing our bad luck would infect them, like a virus.

Our divorce hearing lasted barely fifteen minutes. Who knew that it was so easy to get divorced? Of course, it wasn't easy at all. We sold the boat at a loss. I listed the house, gritting my teeth as I wrote a check for half the amount. My husband took what was not his, claiming he was owed it. I did not have the heart to argue. I was starting over, but this time I was not young.

People began to talk. "I never could understand why you two were together," they said. They outlined the differences between us. They launched into great detail about the strangeness of us, how they never understood why we married in the first place. It should be easy, they said, to move on. Other people did it all the time.

≈

After the divorce, my ex-husband moved away from Alaska. It did not seem possible that we had ever shared a tent high in the mountains, saved each other from falling off a cliff in the fog. He left our house with bitterness and without using the vacuum. Dead leaves and mud coated the carpet like old regrets. His accusations hung in the stale air. I never saw him again.

≈

The day before I left Alaska myself, a stranger came to buy my kayak. I showed him the places it had been damaged and smoothed over. I told him that you couldn't paddle out in the ocean without hitting a few rocks or scraping the boat's flesh now and then. I told him it worked just fine, that unless you looked closely you would never know the difference.

As he looked the kayak over, it did not escape me that I was talking about more than just a boat. I was talking about the hope that I could mend, too, smooth a layer over my heart the same way Wyatt fixed my boat in his kayak shop a few months before he died.

"See here," I said to the buyer. "See this spot, right here on the bow? If you don't look closely, you can't even tell where it was broken." I hoped I was right.

two

The week after I moved out, before my husband left the state for good, I sneaked into my house to gather armloads of gear. I felt like a robber as I moved through the rooms that had once belonged to me. Where had it all gone so wrong? I had thought that maybe I could go back, patch things the way we sometimes fixed our gear, a combination of duct tape and hope. But I knew now this was beyond repair.

I took only the things that were important: my paddle, a Swift carbon-fiber blade that was light as air; my life vest with all its survival items; the dry suit and paddling gloves. The cats. And finally, my yellow kayak, hoisting it up onto the Hully Rollers one last time.

There was a journal beside the bed I had bought, another piece of furniture I had forsaken. Without shame I leafed through it. Maybe here he would dive deeper, to the places he had never shown me, bringing up the secrets he never shared. I flipped to the only written page, hoping that there would be something I could understand—regret, love, hope. But instead, my husband had written that he had met a cute girl, the week I had left him.

I knew then that he would be fine. I wasn't the right woman for him. Perhaps this was the greatest gift, letting him go so he could find her.

The last summer I was in Alaska was full of so much sunshine that I almost changed my mind about leaving. It was a summer for the record books, the sun refusing to give way to the usual clouds. It was a summer when all of us finally used the tubes of sunscreen we had bought years before and had kept in our medicine cabinets ever since. We stripped down to tank tops and shorts. Our skin, unused to the sun, burned in seconds despite our precautions.

Sven muttered about the lack of rain, but most of us reveled in it, although it did feel as though I were naked, unfettered by layers of rain gear. Recklessly, my kayak partners and I kept our rain flies off our tents, staring up through unfamiliar mesh to even more unfamiliar stars above us.

On a set of days off, four friends and I hiked far up into the alpine tundra, reaching a trailless lake still surrounded with snow in July. Icebergs floated lazily on a steel-blue surface. This place was named Lucky Chance, for a mine that had never really panned out, and it seemed appropriate to me, because in a month I would be taking another chance by leaving Alaska for good.

I had found some ocean and mountain friends after all, a tight skein of bright-eyed people who gulped up every adventure they could. With them I had postholed through late snow to the jagged tops of mountains. We had paddled far from town to a thin slice of beach hidden from passing boats, where the soft breath of the ocean entered our dreams. They had stood by me even as I revealed more and more of myself, and hadn't recoiled in horror. I would be sad to leave them, but as all real friends did, they knew why I had to go. There was no ticking clock this time, just the peaceful realization that it was time to leave.

We sat above the lake eating our various pasta dishes and watching a fat sow with two cubs graze high on the mountain slopes above us. Without a rifle between us, we were not worried. This bear was behaving like she was supposed to, staying well away from us, two dogs, and our camp.

As I poured icy water into my granola the next morning, I noticed that the bears had moved farther down the mountain, closer to us than felt right. As I watched, they dropped out of sight into the ravine that separated us. Surely, they would walk the creek out, but a brave member of our party tiptoed over to peek down. He came back high-stepping, his eyes wide. "She is *right there*," he reported.

We milled around anxiously, throwing out suggestions. Retreat? Stand our ground? This was unusual behavior for a bear. It would be better, we decided, to gather in one spot and wait to see what happened. I eyed the younger dog. "Don't worry," my friend said. "She doesn't pay any attention to bears." We gathered near one tent, waiting.

When the bear came up over the ridge and into our camp, she looked enormous. Her muscles rippled under a silky brown coat. The cubs scampered beside her, two round fluffy balls of lighter sable.

The bear hesitated. I knew then that we had taken her presence too casually. The wind had blown our scent away from her, and all this time, she had been unaware of the small group of humans camped below. It was likely, I thought, that she had never seen people before. We represented an unknown danger that she needed to eliminate.

Standing there, I could feel every ounce of me wanting to run. It was a primeval feeling, its flush nearly overpowering me. I could feel the group twitching with the same response. "Hands over our heads," I directed. "We have to look big. Let's all talk to her."

"Hey bear," we chorused in wavering tones. Just then the young dog broke loose and ran at the bear, barking wildly. The bear growled and swiped at the dog, which danced out of the way and raced back toward us.

The bear charged.

In those few seconds, I knew I was facing the fear I had carried with me for years. In my dreams, bears chased me in places just like this, wide-open tundra with nowhere to escape. There were no trees to climb, just unbroken space. The urge to run intensified. Only the knowledge of what would happen if I did kept me rooted in place. I could hear my friends breathing and knew they felt the same way.

Just as survivors of attacks had reported, time slowed down to a trickle. I smelled oatmeal burning in a neglected pot. I could hear the heavy feet as the bear approached at a gallop. I could see long, ivory-colored claws. Despite my fear, I noticed that the bear was beautiful, long strands of chocolate-colored fur catching the early morning sunlight.

About thirty feet from us, the bear skidded to a stop, seemed to reconsider. She angled away from us and stood on her hind legs. Taller than us, she seemed to fill the sky. She made a few feints in our direction and then shook her huge head, collected her cubs, and wheeled away. The three of them galloped down the ravine and out of sight.

I sank to my knees, unable to stand. It had been a close call, the closest I had ever had. I was convinced that if there had been fewer than five of us, the bear would have kept coming. She might have just delivered a warning, one swipe across the face, or she could have mauled us beyond hope. Because the group stood firm, the way I had been trained to do, we had survived.

Somberly we packed up our camp and headed toward salt water. As we walked single file along the backbone of the island, steeply descending to the trees and the ocean and relative safety, I rewound the encounter in my head. There were so many ways it could have ended.

For all of my seven years in Alaska, I had let the fear of bears stalk my days and haunt my nights. Strangely, this encounter erased that fear for good. It was another thing I could finally let go. I never dreamed of bears again.

≈

When I left, I gave away almost everything I owned. I kept only what I thought I would need to pioneer a new life. I was leaving the same way I had arrived, with barely any possessions. I had no idea whether I would stay in the new town I had chosen for one year or twenty. I knew only that it was time to go.

Though this would be my eleventh move as an adult, this felt different from all of the other times. I knew that this time I was not running away. I wasn't looking for the next, better place, propelled by restlessness and desire. This time, I was taking what I had learned with me. I wasn't expecting a place to heal something broken. Alaska had taught me that I really hadn't been broken at all.

There could be, I knew, something besides the two extremes: the road and staying put. You could have a series of homes, all pieces of your heart. None of the ways people called home were better than any others. Although I sometimes envied people like Billy, who knew his piece of ground so deeply, it could be just as good to choose someplace as an adult, just because as you drove over the rounded humps of mountains and into a valley, it felt right. And you didn't even have to lock yourself in and stay the rest of your life. No decisions had to be truly final.

I thought that I resembled the sunshine-colored poppies Jesse and I had found high above Rust Lake. Like them, I was leaving to colonize new ground. Just as I hadn't really known how to settle in one place, or how to be a wife, I had no idea how to start over, alone again. I could only hope I would attempt it with a little more grace and bravery.

I climbed on the same ferry I had arrived on seven years earlier. Eager newcomers streamed off, lugging backpacks and dreams. I wished them well.

A friend waved from shore, her golden hair the only spot of color in a dreary afternoon. Everyone else had already said good-bye and was moving on with life. Squinting from the front deck as the ferry lumbered away, I thought I spotted Rowan in her yellow boat, gliding between the outer islands. A floatplane paced the ferry until it rose higher and disappeared, and I imagined that it held my pilot friend Ron and a pair of new explorers, bound for the coast of Chichagof. Somewhere down by the fish hatchery, my running friends put in the hard miles for another marathon. And Helga, my best friend of the ocean, where was she? It was always hard to tell with her; she could be anywhere. Helga was a survivor.

I swallowed hard as the white buildings of town receded into the lost distance. Alaska had been a place that both broke my heart and mended it again. There were so many ways I could have been a better wife, a more patient kayak partner. Although my husband hadn't wanted to know me, not in the way I wanted to be known, I had tried, and maybe the next time I would get it right. I had wanted home, and I had found it for a little while. I knew now what the Silvies River had always known: there did not have to be a hundred-year flood to be free. You did not have to choose between adventure and home. You could, after all, have both.

When the ferry made the turn that meant this place was irrevocably lost to me, I turned to face what lay ahead, not what was behind.

the layers of the ocean

There are five layers of the ocean, though most of us alive will only ever see one. The deepest layer of the ocean is called by some the midnight zone. The only light comes from bioluminescence, created by animals themselves. In order to see, the creatures there must create their own light. They must move like solitary suns, encased in their own bubbles of freezing water. This layer is the most completely unexplored zone on the planet. Though it is hostile to humans, it is also fascinating beyond belief. If you had a chance to see it, wouldn't you want to go there?

Four years after I left, I came back to Alaska for a visit. I was living far from the sea, and I sometimes missed it with a longing I could nearly taste. Instead of the sea, I had chosen the mountains, climbing high through parched grasses to small alpine lakes. It was just as good, most days. The sun shone with a warmth and intensity I had forgotten was possible. The bears, skittish black ones, remained hidden. The storms, when they came, were predicted by forecasters. You could choose when to go and when to stay without surprise.

I had bought a small plastic kayak, one that would not stand up to the sea, and I took it out on the glacial lake near town, but it wasn't the same. Vacation homes lined the shoreline and boats towing water skiers zoomed past. There was always someone fishing from shore. From the launch, I could see the end of the lake where water met the land. There were no whales, sea otters, or sea lions. There was no mystery. I could lean over in my boat and see the clear rocky bottom, hundreds of feet below. There were no layers to the lake. It was simple and uncomplicated, just what I needed then.

Helga and I met for a hike on a day below zero. She had left her marriage shortly after I did, and our old wounds had mostly healed. We laughed as our boots crunched through the snow, recalling our adventures on the ocean. Wilson the volleyball, the time I forgot the sleeping bag, the time she forgot a raincoat. "Remember the day beds?" I asked. "The guys at the fish weir?" Remember, we said over and over. Remember.

Though neither of us said it, I knew we would never go back, even if we could. It had been good, and then it was done. For the first time, I could look back at the past without trying to recapture it. *What happened?* Finn had asked, but you didn't have to be the person you had been, just because somebody liked you better that way. You could change.

It was just like embarking on a long paddle. You used the landscape as a reference, noting each point as you passed by, looking ahead to the next marker. You folded the chart map down to the next section you needed to navigate. You didn't look back.

Living could be adventure enough. And it was, most of the time. Looking back meant I wasn't paying attention to what was coming next. You could miss a lot that way.

The kayak ranger program lingered on after I left but was slowly fading. There were other things that needed doing, and much more was known about the coast, thanks to us. Volunteers had lined up to do some of the work, people I had once brought along as kayak partners. The money no longer poured in like it used to, and fanciful flights to Whitestripe Lake were a thing of the past.

I never learned whether the poppies Jesse and I diligently recorded at Rust Lake were a different, new species. I didn't really want to know. I hoped they were, and I hoped they still braved the harsh environment they had chosen, tiny new colonies of sunshine.

With nobody to champion its removal, the tunnel under Rust Lake remained in place. In drier summers, the lake drained like a slow bathtub, the ring around its perimeter growing and shrinking with the rain. The pilots still didn't like landing there. Some things would never change.

In the years after I left, a handful of people were killed by bears outside town in separate and puzzling incidents. There was speculation—unusually dry summer, low salmon run—but nobody really had the answers. You could never really read the minds of bears.

Sven retired to the good life, leaving balky motors and insistent kayak ranger whims behind. Others left for the Lower 48, but the people who loved it hung on. They would never live anywhere else. Some of them never could.

The hunting guides persevered through new permit administrators and more boats in their bays. They continued to complain about it but kept going out there. Sometimes I thought they would outlast us all.

In a strange twist of fate, I heard through the coastal telegraph that my old flame Finn had finally followed his dream to Alaska and was living at one of the fish hatcheries along the coast, one of the places I had often visited by boat. I hoped he had found what he was looking for there. But then again, I remembered, you had to bring it with you. Maybe he would be one of the lucky ones.

The missing Beaver floatplane with its five occupants was never found. A psychic had said they were on land, near Catherine Island, one of the places Chance and I had circled on our rescue mission, but if that was the case the forest continued to hold tight to its secrets.

Audrey Sutherland died in 2015. She was ninety years old. I regretted that I had never encountered her in a kayak or camped at the Elves' Hut. I imagined we would have squatted next to a beach fire, going over charts, sharing a bottle of wine. She might have convinced me to worry less and paddle more. I tried to follow her example now. As a woman now much older than the younger ones who streamed into my town with backpacks and dreams, I saw how some of them looked to me as if I knew a few things. Sometimes I felt like the land-based version of Audrey, appearing on the horizon of a trail, headed in a direction that felt certain and sure.

I had thought of the year I left for Alaska in terms of despair, but now I remembered: the same year that the woman drowned in Moon Reservoir, a man was building a rocket. He planned to launch himself into outer space, or as far as he could get, from the hard-packed salt pan called the Alvord Desert.

None of us believed he could do it. How would he breathe, how would he return to earth? In more prosaic terms, we worried about the conse-quences of a forest fire from pieces of fiery rocket falling to earth. Because this was public land, and we were public land managers, we had a stake in what happened. It wouldn't do to have a rocket falling on a tourist under our watch. Despite our concerns, the man labored on. He was convinced of the power of his dream. He believed he could fly, despite all evidence to the contrary, and so he tried. Trying had to be enough, sometimes.

My former husband found a girlfriend with the speed of light in his new town. He had chosen the kind of place he had always wanted to live: metropolitan and safe from gales. He moved on quickly, showing no remorse or regret. From what mutual friends told me, he forsook guns for a new passion, seizing upon it with the same focus as he had done with the old one. I bore him no ill will, although he never understood my departure and refused to believe that it took two people to break apart a marriage in the same way it took two to create it. I hoped that one day he might come to forgive me. I would not lose sleep over it.

I never knew what he did with the kayak I bought him. I hoped he had given it away to someone who would use it and know the magic of the sea. I hoped it did not continue to hang on a wall, covered with moss and regret. Every boat deserved to be paddled, just like every person deserved to be known.

≈

Though I have not paddled a kayak on the ocean in years, I can still remember each stroke. There's the utilitarian forward stroke and the elegant scull, the patient ferry and the determined quarter. I remember Wyatt grinning under the brim of his cap, rain and salt water beading on the bright decks of our boats.

"Stay in the paddler's box," he tells me, and I trust him. In the lake where I paddle, I don't need the brace or the roll. Still, the water can rough up as I turn for home, an unexpected wind ruffling the waves into small whitecaps. It is nothing like what I have known on the Gulf of Alaska, but at those times I remember everything.

I remember Helga and me riding the crest of twelve-foot swells, our boats flexing and dancing as we braced without thinking. I remember those long afternoons, the color of sky matching the color of sea, the forest our backdrop as we moved effortlessly through the forgiving water. I remember slipping into the zone between dreaming and awake, when anything was a possibility, when I could paddle for miles without any effort. I know I could still do all the strokes if I had the chance and the opportunity.

What the ocean taught me was resilience and possibility. Perseverance. Self-reliance. Adaptation. Patience. The list was endless.

What my marriage and its end taught me was to soldier on, despite what the blank spaces on the charts said, the hint of potential disaster contained in each decision. Sometimes you had to keep going through twenty-knot winds, despite the things you had forgotten, despite the mistakes you had made along the way. You had to rescue yourself from these, talk yourself through all the steps you had practiced. Believe.

Just like the ocean, I believe that people have layers too. My husband never let me get past his sunlit zone, the place where there was still light enough to see. I know I needed more than that. I needed to dive deep through the rest of the layers, to know more than what was obvious on the surface.

The last and final layer of the ocean is called the Hadalpelagic Zone. In spite of the near-freezing temperatures and the eternal darkness, creatures still survive there. Humans would be crushed in an instant if by some miracle we could spiral down this far. Though I knew I would never reach this final ocean layer, I thought it might be possible to know someone this genuinely. It would, I thought, be worth the risk.

I know that if my former husband were to write this story, it would be very different. Over the past several years, I have come to see him in a kinder light. Perhaps he realized that there could be more layers than just one. Perhaps he wanted to explore these and wanted to let someone past the easy, sunlit zone. Perhaps he just did not know how. Maybe, if he let her, someone else would be a better teacher than I had been.

In eastern Oregon, in a far different town from the one I had left before moving to Alaska, I relearned the sun and forgot the rain. I found a man who would talk to me, who understood the balance between independence and reliance. We walk that line every day, sometimes well, sometimes not. It has been, in fact, worth the risk. It is home now; I have learned that you accept a place, like you can accept a person, with both its flaws and its brilliance.

In this landlocked town where it rarely rains, I have kept a picture that was taken back in my paddling days. In it, I am facing away from the photographer, floating in a yellow boat. I wear a bright orange life vest and a floppy green rain hat. Naturally, it is raining.

You can see from the dimpled ocean that it is a downpour, but I am at rest, not doing any particular stroke, my paddle across the cockpit. I am looking at a small beach, a break in the wall of forest. A stripe of snow still drapes across it, even though it is June. Three bears—a mother and two cubs—roam the beach, paying no attention to me.

When I look at that picture, I don't see a woman I no longer am. That paddler still moves inside me. Now I know the secret: that you carry with you what you were before and what you will be. There is no expiration date on discovery.

≈

But I miss Alaska. I will always miss Alaska. At night on the edge of sleep and waking, I imagine I am still there. I hear the whisper of rain on the tent fabric, the kiss of water on stone. The salt air paints itself into a film on my lips, my face, my hair. It really was home, though I never truly believed it. In my dreams, I am slipping inside the ocean's skin, one paddle stroke at a time.